Inner Conscious Relaxation

A RENAISSANCE IN CONSCIOUSNESS

Eddie Shapiro was born in New York in 1942. At the age of twenty four he had his first spiritual experience which led him to meeting some of the important spiritual teachers of our time, especially Swami Satchidananda. He was later invited to the Bihar School of Yoga in Monghyr, India, to train with Paramahamsa Satyananda and was initiated as Swami Brahmananda. He has received teachings from His Holiness the Dalai Lama, and His Eminence Tai Situ Rinpoche.

Although Eddie's background finds its roots in traditional Yogic and Buddhist teachings, his understanding comes from a synthesis of both Eastern and Western spiritual realization. Eddie is now living in Boulder, Colorado with his English wife Debbie Shapiro, the well-known author and teacher. Together they teach and share their understanding of spirituality from their own personal experience. They lead workshops *'Clear Mind, Open Heart'* throughout both Europe and America.

Inner Conscious Relaxation

A RENAISSANCE
IN CONSCIOUSNESS

EDDIE SHAPIRO

Edited by Debbie Shapiro

ELEMENT BOOKS

© Eddie Shapiro 1990

First published in Great Britain in 1990 by
Element Books Limited, Longmead, Shaftesbury, Dorset

Cover illustration by Joe Ovies, Image Bank

Cover design by Max Fairbrother

Designed by Roger Lightfoot

Typeset by Burns & Smith Ltd, Derby

Printed and bound in Great Britain
by Billings Ltd, Hylton Road, Worcester

British Library Cataloguing in Publication Data
Shapiro, Eddie
  Inner conscious relaxation: a renaissance in
  consciousness.
  1. Transcendental meditation
  I. Title
  158.12

ISBN 1-85230-164-3

Dedicated to the Truth within all beings

Contents

While we have been happily conquering outer space we have discovered very little about inner space!

However confusing life may be, we are all here together, experiencing the same difficulties. No one is higher or lower than another, no matter what their position or status in life. The king, president, beggar and thief are all part of the same reality. I felt this strongly when my wife, Debbie, and I met the Dalai Lama. Debbie went to touch his feet in the traditional manner, but he made her stand up, saying, 'We are all equal here.' Yes. We all breathe the same air and share the same world. If a rich man and a poor man were both held under water, we could guarantee that their only thoughts when emerging would be for breath, not for riches or wealth! As the nineteenth-century American philosopher Emerson put it, 'As long as our civilization is essentially one of property, of fences, of exclusiveness, it will be mocked by delusions. Our riches will leave us sick; there will be bitterness in our laughter; and our wine will burn our mouths. Only that good profits which we can taste with all doors open, and which serves all men.' The ignorance of duality, of believing we are all separate from each other, is buried in our own minds, and it is necessary to break through this illusion in order to experience real understanding.

Situations are simultaneously both local and global: whatever affects us personally also affects the whole, and individually we are each a part of a collective consciousness that embraces this. The way in which we react to stresses and tensions is a major issue and it is growing as we enter the 1990s, for stressful emotions and attitudes are the root of most negativity: they throw us off-balance and we become less able to function fully. The causes of stress in our lives are innumerable. By 1992 there will be over 5 billion people living together on this planet and we are all influencing each other, even if we are not aware of it. We live in a world reduced in apparent size by our ability to communicate anywhere and everywhere instantly through modern technologies; simul-taneously there is deep misunderstanding that keeps us in chaos, confusion and fear of each other. At the same time the ozone layer is decaying, the rain forests are diminishing, animal species are becoming endangered, our atmosphere and oceans are polluted; our mental institutions are full.

True change comes from within

Within all this chaos we want to be or to go somewhere else, but wherever we go there we are! Our world is not something we can escape from too easily, for it is simply an extension of ourselves, a reflection of our understanding. And how can we be at peace with our world if we are not at peace with ourselves? We play so many roles, we act out so many parts in our attempt to find out who we are. These then smother us with labels – I am this, I am that, I am something, I am nothing – rather than just being a living, breathing, wonderful human, for whom life is a precious gift. Our dissatisfaction makes us desperate for change, but we do not know how to bring about the deeper change that we are really craving for. So we change the superficial things. We have a facelift, breast implant, tummy tuck or hair transplant – all sorts of changes so that people will admire us and be attracted to us, will want us. All we want is to be wanted! But if we change our lives from within then the outer beauty will also transform, for it is the neurosis within us that distorts the outer appearance. We need to go deeper, within ourselves. Then our outside world too will appear different. Deep, conscious relaxation is one way to contact that part of our being that initiates this process.

When we are at peace with ourselves we have no desire to fight one another. People are at war with each other as we are at war within ourselves. Individual stress soon becomes collective stress, and then planetary stress. Whatever we are experiencing directly affects those around us. Our confusion and difficulty in understanding this is due to seeing ourselves as isolated from each other, locked into our own limited experiences. We are not aware of how inter-dependent and connected every being is to each other; we do not even know how to go beyond the reality we have created around us.

We are naturally free but, because we are motivated by our unconscious drives and the limitations in our understanding, that freedom is quickly lost. We have been accumulating impressions and opinions about what life should be like since before birth. The various stresses that lie deep within all of us cause us to act as we do, as the vast unconscious is far more influential than our conscious mind is aware. Even a murderer acts out of unconscious convictions, driven by what he or she believes to be true. In the East they say the mother is the first teacher or guru; her unconditional love enables us to feel nourished and wanted. But if the mother has suffered from abuse or neglect, then can we expect her to be a loving mother to her children? And if we are abused as children, is it not possible that we will enter life presuming the world to be an abusive place, and will we not be on a constant alert to attack?

Religion offers codes of behaviour that can help us understand what is right conduct, encouraging us to be better people. The Buddha taught, 'If right thought is kept well in the mind, no evil thing can ever enter there.' A moral life enables us to achieve full growth, mental stability and an understanding compatible with living together. However, many contrary issues can arise, causing indifference and anger. Some religions we have relied on for guidance, born in the name of love and equality, spend their time fighting with each other; they are deluded into believing that one way is better than another. Organized religion has become form without life, it has a lack of spontaneity and a lifeless unreasonableness, and it offers few positive examples for us to follow. So we lose trust in the teachings.

This lack of personal faith in, and understanding of, ourselves is a further stress-related factor. From stress soon comes distress. The inability to look within for answers creates panic and anxiety about our future: we think that something or someone out there will determine our fate. Our future is something we dread, for we are all impermanent – at some point we know we will die. But as death is in the future we prefer to avoid dealing with our feelings about it, and instead we hold on to the past. We carry our past around with us – all our guilt, shame, anger and resentment. We are thus influenced by issues from the past and by a fear of the future. We become self-centred, uncaring about what happens to others as long as we ourselves are all right. We lose touch with the basic qualities of giving and compassion as our fear of external events and the effect they may have on us creates deep tension. The pain we feel in ourselves we then blame on others.

Cause and effect

Unless we can look at these problems and difficulties with a relaxed mind, then all we do is create more pain. A tense mind creates chaos, while a calm and clear mind creates sensitive and positive solutions. A dysfunctional person creates a dysfunctional world. When we are stressed, everything becomes an irritation (a distress). In our ignorance we misunderstand the beauty of life, making objects and possessions more important. Friendships are lost and families are broken because of desire and greed. Once in a stressful state we begin to look outside ourselves for reinforcement or help, perhaps in the form of alchohol, drugs or therapy, as the pressure becomes too much to bear.

By becoming at ease we can have a positive effect on others and the world we live in. When we are at peace nothing can disturb us. This is the basic law of karma, that as we think so we become, that nothing stands independent but all causes have an effect and all effects have a cause. This teaches us directly that we are responsible for our own actions and whatever reaction there may be to those actions. It is not just an intellectual understanding, but a natural law that applies everywhere. If we can make a shift in our awareness then we can move away from greed and selfishness towards generosity and compassion, for we can see the effect these qualities can have. By re-educating our minds life becomes a great and precious gift, rather than a worrisome burden.

Many of us have gone on inner journeys or some sort of quest, looking for answers to our own stresses and that of the world as a whole. We may have travelled to the East and sought guidance; we have met with masters and received teachings; or we have spent time going to seminars and workshops. During my own quest is how I first discovered Inner Conscious Relaxation.

The consciousness-expanding revolution

I grew up in New York in the 1950s. There had always been a sense of unconsciousness and frustration in the city: a feeling of being troubled, closed, unfriendly, withdrawn, even anti-social. People would walk along the crowded streets with sad and lonely faces, and there was constant tension between the various ethnic groups. Immigrants had come to New York from all over the world to compete and make money: America was a land of prosperity, and everyone wanted a piece of the apple. But these people preferred to stick to their own roots and they brought with them their own cultures to reimplant in their new world. This led to racial discrimination and the setting up of all sorts of barriers, adding to the tension of an already overcrowded place.

By the late 1960s I had noticed a development taking place in myself and the people around me. A new, opposing energy was evolving and it was growing in greater proportion. It was seen as a consciousness-expanding revolution, or the beginning of the 'love generation'. A vibrant energy combined with a great surge of creativity: different art forms and music were flourishing and taking on new dimensions. At this time I began to meet various people who were to become not only lifelong friends but also dynamic influences in the direction of this new wave of consciousness.

At first we created a communal lifestyle in the heart of New York. We pooled our money and assisted each other, working as artists, dancers and so on. We became vegetarians; we began reading esoteric books and learning the various teachings of yoga, Zen and Buddhism. We read Alan Watts, Ralph Waldo Emerson and Henry David Thoreau, the philosophers and transcendentalists. These were new and stimulating, causing us to delve deeper, to find out more of their meaning. But we were also feeling a need for a teacher, someone who was already established in himself and was a living example of all that the books were trying to say. Throughout the written word a message prevailed that went to the heart of the matter: 'When the student is ready the teacher appears.' We had already begun our process of transformation, but as yet had no teacher; and in those days it seemed as if there were very few real teachers around.

After a while we moved out into the countryside, to a farm where we could take what we were learning a step further. We found a beautiful place and called it the Walden Yoga Farm, named after Thoreau's book. Although we lived simply, problems arose out of this need for a guide, for someone who was more knowledgeable about how to live and grow in a spiritual community. Our unevolved consciousness, redolent of past ignorance, was beginning to lose importance. The desire to be competitive and the search for pleasure were diminishing. We wanted to simplify our lives and devote our time to exploring within, but we lacked direct guidance.

When reading various yoga books I realized that what I was going through was a state known as 'vairagya', dispassion. The things of the world were losing their importance, and I was in need of expression that was not limited by mere worldly pleasures. I needed, as we all do at various times in our lives, to find deeper meaning and a more significant reason to exist. An inner joy was leading me to profound experiences, but it all seemed so contrary to the life I had grown up in that it was hard to know what was real and what was fantasy. I had been a kid on the streets of New York, avoiding street fights, going to high school dances - and now I was getting a calling?

Then a friend told me about a holy man who had come to New York from India. He was a Swami, a master who taught yoga, and apparently he radiated joy and peace wherever he went. At that time it was an unheard of idea (at least in most of America) that happiness could be found by looking within; that by relaxing and quieting the mind people could experience peace or bliss surpassing anything physical or mental. To think or say such things was too esoteric, too mystical. In fact a Swami was always depicted looking into a crystal ball, and a yogi would have his legs wrapped around his neck in contorted positions, as if he were showing off. It still seemed that for someone to have a good time and enjoy himself it was necessary to go to a fancy hotel or a good movie!

We went to see this Swami. He had a long beard, long hair and wore saffron-coloured robes. It was an extraordinary moment for us, because when you meet an awakened being the most incredible changes take place. The true masters emanate peace, tranquillity, loving kindness, warmth and bliss that is inescapable and irresistible. They are magnetic.

You feel drawn to them from deep down inside. Swami Satchidananda was the first holy man I had ever met, and the first being I had ever encountered who radiated these qualities.

It was a tremendous affirmation, as my background had never permitted or encouraged this type of understanding. Life in the 1950s was very superficial; people were judgmental and had all sorts of prejudices: Jews against Catholics, and everyone against Blacks or Puerto Ricans. We were respected because of our accomplishments or financial success, what kind of car we drove, where we had travelled to or who we knew. Fighting was accepted as a necessary part of life. To look a little deeper, to go within and discover ourselves, was unthinkable; it was even something to be ridiculed.

As changes began taking place in me and I acquired new insights, my old scepticism, doubt and confusion began to dissolve. Before meeting Swami Satchidananda it seemed hard to believe that the divine qualities were for everyone. God was somewhere far away and was watching every move we made, counting our sins and our merits. But that meeting with the Swami was enough to make me see that the divine qualities, that all that was good, could be realized, could be experienced within ourselves. His very nature was able to reflect the God within me.

I had never before met anyone who was all-embracing or seemed to really know the deeper meaning of life. His depth was infinite; looking into his eyes I sensed I could see eternity. It felt like no one was home. I began to realize that this state I was experiencing in him was pure egolessness. His very existence was for others, and he expressed this in all his actions, talks and teachings. He particularly taught that leading an unselfish life is the most rewarding path to follow, because desire is an endless chain that never breaks and can only bring pain. As long as we are not attached to the desire, we can be free. To lead a dedicated life can bring joy and unsurmountable happiness.

These teachings were given to us in numerous ways. We started to go to yoga classes, learning hatha yoga and pranayama (postures and breathing exercises); purifying our bodies and cleansing our minds, developing our concentration. It was not easy at first. It seemed to me, as a New Yorker, that these teachings were alien to the Western way of life and therefore challenges always arose. But Swamiji* was very patient and allowed us to progress naturally. I began spending more and more time engaged in my practice, determined to make my life a reflection of these higher ideals.

It was then that I met another great teacher, one of Swami Satchidananda's guru brothers, Swami Satyananda, who was visiting New York from India while on a world tour. Still a novice, I was unsure what to expect and our first meeting was very short. After dinner I was asked to escort him to his car. As we walked along he seemed very different from the Swami whom I was used to. Swami Satchidananda was tall and graceful, gentle and sensitive in his manner, while Swami Satyananda was short and solid, precise and blunt. He said that Swami Satchidananda was a loving father, but that he himself was a military captain! That statement, and other times I personally spent with him, sparked a longing to go to India to be with him and study further. I wanted to see how this ancient Indian culture differed from my ingrained New York conditioning, and I knew that if I was to work with myself further I needed more teachings. So when Swami Satyananda invited me to his ashram † in Bihar, I was ready to go.

It was 1968. People all over the USA were going through radical changes. The need to go back to the land to 'tune in and drop out' had become the popular slogan. I had met Tim Leary, Allen Ginsberg, Richard Alpert (who is now known as Ram Dass), and various other contemporaries who were influencing the consciousness of so many, but I wanted to find out for myself the root of what was taking place. So when folks began heading West to San Francisco with 'flowers in their hair', I headed East.

---

* Swamiji is a term of endearment meaning 'dear Master' or 'dear teacher'

† an ashram is a spiritual community

Finding the way

When I first arrived at Swami Satyananda's Bihar School of Yoga there were only a few people there. It was a simple place with modest accommodation: a men's and a women's dormitory, an outside kitchen area, an office and a large meditation hall. It was my first experience of a traditional ashram and I felt it to be the perfect setting for what I had come to do. I stayed and poured my heart into a whole new way of being.

What this journey ultimately taught me was, no matter how hard we practise, no matter how many teachers we go to, unless we are truly relaxed we cannot progress. Our forward motion is handicapped by our own ability to go within and ease the stressful state of our subconscious and unconscious minds, our inner stresses. All of our past and present actions are registered there, which then determines our motivations and actions. To release these energies we need to probe so deep that the buried impressions can begin to surface; we explode these patterns by probing into the boundlessness that is beyond the content of the mind. It was that boundlessness that I saw in my teacher.

It is as if we are stuck and do not know which way to turn. We are surrounded by an enormous number of techniques and methods, all promising prosperity, healing and enlightenment. But in our everyday lives we are immersed in confusion to the point where we have forgotten why we are here, and what the deeper purpose of this life is. We have become self-centred and involved with our own salvation, success and abundance, so that we have lost touch with the true teachings: those that remind us of simplicity, humility, grace and compassion. And we have forgotten that whatever path we follow is personal and makes little difference. The only importance is for true change to happen from inside ourselves. We cannot love another when we have not yet learnt to love ourselves. When we start at home then we are able to purify our minds, to become selfless and truly giving. Ultimately selfless actions bring the highest understanding. When our motivation is clear then the desire to give, help and care for others arises naturally, as does the tolerance to accept all different paths and ways of being.

What we do between birth and death is our path, our journey, different for each one of us. Few of us feel comfortable in this world or in this body – most of us are, in fact, strangers to ourselves. Yet if we don't know how to live with ourselves in a whole and accepting way, how can we expect to live peacefully with others? Life is too short and precious to be dismissed as unimportant. I remember when I was a child how an adult of twenty seemed really old; then, when I was twenty, forty seemed old; and now at forty-seven it all seems to pass in a flash!

Caretakers of ourselves and of the earth

Although life is so elusive and we may not be able to grasp the true nature of things in an all-encompassing way, we can do our best to make this world a better place. Through awareness and mindfulness we can be caretakers here, taking a joyful responsibility for both ourselves and the planet. The earth has been described as a living organism, and as caretakers we can therefore work together to keep it healthy. It is not always an easy task as we are each so different, yet together we partake in the earthly drama! There is a need for an inner conscious renaissance, one that encourages freedom and higher ideals. If we understand that this life, this breath, is a gift, a great treasure, then just being alive becomes a joy. As long as we have breath we are an important part of this creation. More of us are now sharing this feeling and want to explore, to understand and to know the various paths that enable us to deepen our perception of truth, to experience personally the different dimensions of consciousness.

In this way we can begin to answer our question, 'Why are we here?' We know how to build spaceships and war machines, but so often fail to go deep enough within ourselves to deal effectively with stress. Is it our purpose simply to suffer, or can we go beyond the suffering? Is it not our responsibility, both to ourselves and to others, to become aware of this? It can be such a wonderful adventure. The rewards are ease, acceptance of self, freedom and greater understanding of purpose. All the answers are within our reach, if we can be fearless enough to explore and confront ourselves.

To act fearlessly means letting go of the fixed images we

have of ourselves, particularly the false belief that we cannot change. It means to go beyond fear so we do not hide from who we are but can confront it and be brave. It means opening ourselves joyfully to whatever may happen. As we accept ourselves, change happens naturally. It is as if we can become warriors, our enemies being the negative forces in our minds, and our weapons being love and compassion. The teaching of Ahimsa, (which means non-violence or harmlessness in Sanskrit), to both ourselves and others, is very beneficial to help us live fearlessly. Non-violence is beautifully exemplified by both Mahatma Gandhi and by His Holiness the Dalai Lama, who was recently awarded the Nobel Peace Prize because of his non-violent actions towards the Chinese. These great men have shown that the power of compassion is greater than that of the sword. 'The best soldier does not attack,' wrote the ancient Chinese philosopher Lao Tzu. 'The superior fighter succeeds without violence. The greatest conqueror wins without struggle. This is called intelligent non-aggressiveness. This is called mastery of men.'

When we can relax deeply and experience true peace, then these words of wisdom become obvious to us and bring about great transformation. Then we become the masters of our own beings, instead of the slaves. When we can contact the sanity and goodness within, then we can see how we are really an instrument of genius. By simply getting to the root cause of confusion we begin to reflect a higher ideal and to manifest true compassion. By discovering our purpose we release an abundant store of creative energies. Then there can be constructive answers to our world state, real inner peace and a deepening of conscious awareness and awakening.

2

The
Distress
of Stress

Is it not extraordinary that one of the most stressful situations in life is human relationships? Our egos are constantly butting into each other, causing tension - our way of doing things versus someone else's way, and the need to hold on to what we think is the right way. Our individual likes and dislikes, attractions and repulsions, various mood swings, unconscious motivations and influences can all create barriers to communicating clearly and freely. Communication can be so difficult. We misunderstand each other and conflicts easily arise; what we say is not always what we mean. Or we hide behind our inhibitions, not knowing how to be honest about what we are really feeling, and our limitations continually hold us back from expressing ourselves openly. All our own personal issues are compounded with the expectations we put on each other and the demands of being a best friend or lover, parent or child, causing confusion and misunderstanding. We put so much time and energy into relationships, yet they so often let us down, creating tremendous distress.

When we were with the Dalai Lama in his palace in India, we were delighted to discover such a simple and amusing man. His friendliness, unassuming manner, warmth, sense of humour and tremendous compassion, as well as the fact that we were so fortunate to be alone with him, all made me spontaneously say to him, 'I don't want to leave. I want to be with you all the time!' He laughingly replied, 'If we were together all the time we would quarrel!' I was both surprised and relieved at such a reply; surprised because it is easy to forget how very ordinary such a extraordinary man as this can be; and relieved because Debbie and I were on our honeymoon, and if I could quarrel with His Holiness then I could certainly quarrel with my wife! This meeting was a great lesson in human relationships, for we are social animals and the need to come together lies deep within us, however hard it may be.

Without personal relationships the loneliness that develops can be the greatest of hardships. We are all alone in this world, but that is not the same as being lonely. Being alone can be a very creative state, a feeling of comradeship and unity with all life. Being lonely is a feeling of being separate from life, which can lead to despair, depression and even psychosis. Loneliness is born out of the desire to share on an intimate level, to be held and loved and reassured that our place in this world is a safe one. When this need is not fulfilled it leaves us feeling empty and isolated. On a higher level this is because we believe we have become separated from God, for if God is everywhere and in all things then ideally we can never be lonely. But on a human level the need to share with someone our ups and downs, our sensitive, weak and tender moments, can bring to the surface all our feelings of inadequacy and insecurity, creating personal distress. And how hard it is, when we are feeling sad or depressed, to be able to appreciate another's happiness or success, for this simply highlights our own lack.

Stress is nothing new. Ever since man has been on this planet he has encountered stressful situations, such as when the caveman had to cope with the daily reality of finding food and deal with the fight-or-flight dilemma when confronting wild animals; or when the farmers and fishermen had to learn to live with droughts and storms, or in the constant human predicament of love and the loss of love. These stress-producing factors may be different, but they have the same effect on the body. It's amazing that thousands of years later man is not extinct and that the human race is still racing, since distress factors have so alarmingly increased!

The nature of the mind

The human mind is complex. As individuals we know so little
about how it works. When we have a problem we don't know
how to deal with then we go to professionals to get diagnosed,
to find out if we are neurotic, psychotic, schizophrenic or
manic depressive. We take prescribed drugs to ease the pain,
or we undergo therapy. We are so ignorant about this
beautiful instrument, our mind; we have such a limited
concept of how it works, or even how to use it. We are
strangers to our own mind, ignorant of something we live
with our whole lives, acting out its commands, fulfilling its
desires. Yet we have no idea how to delve deeper to discover
the depths and magnitude of this extraordinary part of our
being.

To learn how to expand, nourish, make friends with and
enjoy ourselves can bring great happiness and creativity.
Without this understanding our energies can so easily become
scattered. The constant mental chatter and distractions, the
various tensions, external and internal overloads, all create
distress. We must first learn how to tame this mind for it has
many different tendencies: sometimes it is like a monkey
bitten by a scorpion, while at other times it can be like a gentle
lamb. It fluctuates and disperses energy without our having
any control over the matter. Just as we care for our body we
can learn to care for our mind, to keep it clean, productive
and useful.

When a mind becomes stressed it acts out of this painful
state. And when we are confronted with obstacles it feels as if
we are facing an invisible, impenetrable wall for our minds
can find no way through the pain. A stressed mind creates
barriers that seem impossible to deal with and buries itself in
more and more delusion. We are influenced by what people
think and feel; we react to simple issues as if they were matters
of life and death; we are unsure and uncertain what to do with
ourselves or how to make decisions; and we easily become
angry or upset. Is it not because our minds are scattered and
confused, unable to focus, influenced by past traumas, that
we do not know how to trust ourselves or be spontaneous?

Have you ever noticed how the chatter in our heads can go
on endlessly, flitting from one subject to another, creating

fantasies and acting out dramas? We get into conversations with ourselves and spend an enormous amount of our time preoccupied with this mental phenomenon. This disperses our energy, leading us in so many different directions, until we begin to feel distressed. Most of us take it for granted that this is the way it is. We over-analyze and get immersed in questioning ourselves. Our insecurities, doubts and fears keep this mental chatter alive. As our energies become scattered we get more depressed, often neurotic; we can even lose grip with reality and soon we are out of control. In this way the distress of stress easily affects us.

Few of us actually know how to deal with stress, unless it becomes acute and we need medical assistance. Instead we avoid it, deny it, hope it will go away, or we become distracted by mindless activities like going to parties, watching television or eating gourmet meals. We get involved with the lives of the rich and famous, becoming absorbed with anything that will help us side-step our own problems, anything that will distract us even temporarily. We love the dreamlike and exotic world of others and immerse ourselves in the lives of politicians, royalty and movie stars, becoming indignant, sad or elated depending on their fate. We even believe that if we know or meet a famous person we will feel better about ourselves!

Yet these pastimes do little more than dull the mind; they lack real inspiration. Sitting in an easy chair with our feet up and entertaining ourselves has become synonymous with relaxation, as has the great luxury of saving up all year to go on holiday. The problem is that we invariably don't get the rest and relaxation we bargained for. What really happens is that we stay at the party a little too long or argue a few times too many, and we come home exhausted! We are in a hurry, rushing through life as if we are running for shelter during a storm and therefore we become nervous and irritated. Having rushed to work, rushed to eat and rushed to sleep, we become overburdened and tense. Then we rush to the Mediterranean or the Caribbean to go on holiday!

But wherever we go or whatever we do, along come all our inner stresses. Irritation, mood changes and depression lurk behind our every action. A selfish mind causes tension, is untrusting and unaware; greed is all-pervasive and very deluding. We have become obsessed with prosperity and abundance and see them as synonymous with contentment and freedom. So when we do not get them we become stressed and feel we have somehow failed. Beneath it all we really do want true happiness, but we get lost in our fleeting attempts at looking for it.

The battlefield of stress

In the great Indian epic the *Bhagavad Gita*, known as the Song of God, we see a man in deep distress concerning his family. The warrior Arjuna is confronted with having to fight on a great battlefield. But he sees that relatives on both sides are at war with each other and is distraught about what to do. This story has been compared to the war within each one of us, the conflicting aspects of our personalities at war with each other. The higher good is at battle with our lower, more negative forces; our minds are in a state of confusion. The life within is a battlefield, with our fears, neurosis, frustrations, prejudices, pain and anguish all fighting for our attention.

This struggle reveals the built-in stress that has preyed on man's ignorance throughout the ages. In our distress a kind of hopelessness seems to prevail. It is easier to follow in past footsteps, to go through life in a semi-conscious way, for this demands little conscious thought. So we go on building sandcastles in the sky. But what is it to live? To be? To see? To be free? Day by day we are striving for fulfilment, satisfaction and entertainment. We want a way out, so we search for things to keep us busy. We become workaholics and alcoholics. We are addicted to life, but we have not yet discovered how to live it in a free and spontaneous way.

The distress or confusion we experience is symbolic of our struggle in life and the choices we make. The greed within, the need to accumulate, the desire for power and control, all have their effects. As we are stressed, so our world is in distress. Our values are based on selfish motives and false ideals and so we suffer. The truth is concealed, it is difficult to live up to our highest good and we are stuck in mediocrity.

Stress is the number one killer in the world today. *Time* magazine wrote in 1989:

> Two-thirds of office visits to family doctors are prompted by stress-related symptoms. Stress-related absenteeism, company medical expenses and lost productivity (in America) may cost between 50–75 billion (US dollars) a year. Stress is now known to be a major contributor, either directly or indirectly, to six of the leading causes of death in the US, namely coronary heart disease, cancer, lung ailments, accidental injuries, cirrhosis of the liver, and suicide. The three best-selling prescription medications in the US (Valium, Inderal and Tagament) treat problems either caused or aggravated by stress, namely anxiety, hypertension and ulcers.

Stress weaves it way into every avenue of our lives. Whoever we are, it constricts us. Frustration, insecurity, fear and aimlessness are the most common factors that turn stress into distress. Each year 32 billion lbs of aspirin, 5 million downers, 3 million uppers and 5 million tranquilizers are consumed! We have explored and exhaused so many areas of life, but haven't learnt how to alleviated the distress from within.

The biochemical effects of stress in the body

When we first begin to experience psychological stress an alarm is sounded in the brain. This initial stress factor may be as simple as the recollection of a painful memory, or someone shouting at us. If the event has any threatening nature about it, then the brain is activated. The hypothalamus is a small part of the brain in an area known as the limbic system, and it is here that the alarm sounds: the stress response.

The limbic system is known as the seat of emotions in man, for it is within this area of the brain that our emotional states and responses are registered; this system also monitors many of our bodily functions, thereby linking the effect of stress with our physical responses. For instance, the hypothalamus regulates the autonomic nervous system which in turn regulates our heart rate, digestion and metabolism, blood pressure, respiration and reproduction. When the alarm is sounded this whole area is affected. It is therefore hardly surprising that stress leads to heart problems, excessive sweating, digestive disorders, ulcers, impotence and so on.

The sympathetic nervous system is that which prepares us for action in the fight-or-flight syndrome. It involves the secretion of particular hormones. But when the fight-or-flight problem is not actually life-threatening, even though our bodies respond to it with stress signals, we then have to deal with the excess hormones left in our system. The body becomes weakened by dealing with the stress response, and it has less resistance.

The stress response affects us in three stages: firstly an alarm sounds in the brain; this is followed by a period of resistance in which we do not necessarily feel the effect of the stress on a conscious level; and finally there is exhaustion, when the body cannot cope any longer. Physiological stress pertains to the effect of stress on the body – the nervous system, the muscles and hormone balance. The symptoms that arise are rarely released through normal relaxation circumstances such as watching television or going on holiday. Emotional stresses arise out of the opposites, such as love and hate, profit and loss, success and failure, happiness and unhappiness. The effects of these stresses are even harder to resolve because we find it so difficult to express our emotions freely or openly. We bottle up all of our conflicts and they become buried in our unconscious. Mental stresses are the result of excessive mental activity, creating a jumble of thoughts, confusions and delusions. This is the hardest of all to resolve, especially in normal circumstances, for we are too immersed in such chaos to find our way out on a conscious level. We have to go beyond the conscious mind (as in Inner Conscious Relaxation) to be able to resolve stress on this level.

The physical results of excessive stress can include the following: headaches, diarrhoea, high blood pressure, grinding teeth, palpitations, hyperventilation, disturbed sleep, backache, loss of appetite, asthma, skin rashes, peptic ulcers, excessive sweating, chest pains, dry mouth, hives, restlessness, pacing, fidgeting and nail-biting. Psychological symptoms may include disturbing moods such as depression, anger, inappropriate and excessive elation, rapid or dramatic mood changes, anxiety, addictive behaviour such as excessive eating or sudden weight loss, impaired concentration, loss of memory, confusion, irrational fears, indecisiveness, self-consciousness, disorganization, ideas of injuring oneself or others, changes in appearance such as sloppy dressing, poor self-care, stuttering, stammering, halting speech, impotence, sexual promiscuity, phobias, marital problems and children's behaviour problems.

The nature of stress

Our very being is built from stress, so it is impossible to avoid it. As soon as the first cells of life begin to divide a dynamic tension is set up, as there is more than one cell present. Even when we are asleep we are experiencing some form of stress, as the body has to continue to function. However, stress itself is not really the issue. It is our reaction to an event, thought or demand made upon us that is important and which determines either a pleasant or painful experience. In other words, stress is not an independent entity that we have to suffer – it is simply the result of the way in which we handle our lives. It makes no difference what the stress-producing factor may be, it is the way we react to those factors that is essential. Stress may therefore include joyful and stimulating experiences if we respond in such a way; while distress is always difficult and even damaging, as it is the result of a negative reaction to stress.

How we deal with a situation therefore determines the effect that that situation has in us. Our reactions are often the result of what we find buried in our past, for we become conditioned to react to situations in a set way, each time triggering off the inner alarm signal. And all of our past traumas and experiences are recorded in the unconscious. There they make impressions, called 'samskaras'.* These unconscious and subconscious impressions are constantly influencing our conscious mind, determining how we make decisions or why we behave in certain ways. They hold us in

* A Sanskrit word meaning mental impressions that influence us on an unconscious and subconscious level.

fixed patterns of behaviour and create the limitations and delusions we have to deal with if we are to become free and spontaneous.

The language we use can add to our negative attitudes. For instance, when we constantly repeat words such as terrible, awful, frightful, miserable, or other such negatives, we are imposing a pattern in the mind. Phrases that are in common use in our language do the same thing, giving the mind and body an impression of fear or threat. Phrases like, 'I can't stand it,' or 'It's killing me', or 'This is going to be the death of me', start having a literal effect and can set off the alarm. It is irrelevant whether the threat actually exists or not. It is the internal response that sets the stress reaction in motion.

Tension can therefore be seen as resulting from our experience of the relationship between ourselves and our environment; how we react to the events in our lives, how we feel we are being treated, if we are helpless or in control. This relationship is based on the preservation of our ego, so it is naturally biased. It puts ourselves first at all times and represents the expectancy that bad things are going to happen to us, followed by our doubt that we will be able to deal with them. We therefore desire to keep things as they are rather than allowing change to occur, for change appears as a threat and creates stress. When we are willing and open to change and allow it to take place freely, then it can become a joyful challenge and does not have the same stressful effect.

However, since early childhood we are raised to believe that we have to confront the world and succeed. To do so we have to have control over our reality, and control of this nature does not allow for change. So then we have to deal with the stress response that occurs when change does take place. The 'I have to win' factor starts with our toys and the games we play. It becomes a dominant part of growing up. Our friends admire us if we excel in sports, we become more popular if we are the class athlete or win a contest. Who we are as human beings is secondary to how much we possess, what our position in life is and who we know. We cannot all win, have great wealth, be the best-looking or most popular, for the world is based on inequality. This contributes to an unhealthy society. Failure can lead to mental anguish, severe depression, feelings of inadequacy and even suicide. There is not enough emphasis put on the human aspect of life. Instead we are primed to compete and to win. The rewards for success are numerous, but the heartache of failure is painful and we have difficulty trying to deal with this. In this way we can feel tremendous loneliness and a lack of belief or trust in ourselves.

One of the most confusing issues to deal with in ourselves is our relationship to anger. Although anger causes us great distress physically, mentally and emotionally, there are different schools of thought on how to approach it. Most Western psychologists think it is good to release anger because when it is suppressed it can build up, creating unconscious and damaging patterns of behaviour. However, anger is painful to those on whom it is vented, disturbs our own peace of mind and can generate even more anger. Constant anger causes great harm and can become an ingrained habit, continually feeding upon itself. Expressing our anger may have an immediately satisfying response, but anger is invariably based on our ego having been affronted or insulted in some way and this is a never-ending drama. Many great teachers, including the Dalai Lama, believe that anger of any sort is basically destructive, that instead of expressing it we should get to the root of the anger, through self-investigation and work on resolving the issue there.

Acknowledging our impermanence

Our time in this world is so temporary, yet our egotistic mind makes us think and act as if we will live forever. We like to believe that death only happens to others, and that if it does exist for us, it is somewhere in the far-off future. It is only when we are confronted by the death of a close friend or relative, or a serious illness or accident ourselves, that we are clearly faced with the reality of impermanence. Yet nothing in life is permanent. The thoughts and cares we had yesterday may not even pertain to today, however much energy we may put into dealing with them.

So our lives are spent trying to solidify, to hold on to, to make secure our existence, whether it be possessions, people and relationships, thoughts, ideas, or even dreams – yet at any moment the rug can be pulled from under us. No matter who we are, our lives are impermanent. There are no guarantees, there is no real security; the only security is in knowing that there is none. Man is the only creature which lives in so much confusion. We make decisions every day that we regret and wish we could change. Indecisiveness and wanting things to be different inevitably creates greater confusion. We make plans, but the events of the world and the possibility of change are always shifting and affecting us. I often ponder upon what John Lennon said: 'Life is what's happening when we are planning other things.' If we cannot be spontaneous then we inevitably suffer distress, for our minds and the world we live in are constantly shifting. If we can see and accept this as true, then we begin to see ourselves and our reality more clearly. The great teacher Swami Satchidananda says, 'Make no appointments, then there are no disappointments!' When we are free of expectations and of wanting results, then we can be free of confusion and tension.

Man has tended to use aggression as a means to solve problems: might makes right. Instead of looking for peaceful solutions we have looked the opposite way, towards aggressive means. Through ignorance we have acquired a destructive nature and possessive attitude, and we impose these attitudes on others for our own purposes. This behaviour passes from one generation to the next, and in this way stress and related patterns become addictions in themselves. The dysfunctional* family, the twelve-step programme and issues concerning co-dependency have all become major topics in the past few years as we begin to realize how deep our level of denial really is.

We enter life as a baby, and to become an adult we have to go through a process of maturing. To grow in this way means taking responsibility and having the willingness to learn and discover for ourselves. Yet we seem to have so little time to investigate what is really happening in the most important

* Families with addictive and psychological problems based on negative habitual behavioural patterns.

area of all, inside ourselves. We even joke and put someone down by saying, 'He's real deep,' as if a depth of understanding was a social impairment. Are we not here to enjoy the real wealth? Are mediocrity and superficiality our rewards for growing old? We come into this life crying as babies and most of leave crying and are still babies, not having truly learnt how to mature.

But all is not lost! We have looked at how the negative force of distress impairs this great gift of life; the pain of relationships, the sadness due to loneliness, the scars of the past and our inability to understand how our minds work. Yet life need not be such a hopeless mess! It is workable. We just have to find out how to use some of the keys that unlock the vast treasures within. The way through is there if we want to take it. The various spiritual teachings are available to us all. They describe how to live in this world and to discover the joy of our true nature, how to act in a mature and thoughtful way, how to overcome our selfish and egotistical demands. They speak of generosity and non-attachment, qualities of gratitude and selflessness. They explain how we can live peacefully in the world without causing harm or distress to others.

The wisdom from these teachings is not based on intellectual understanding but is a living truth discovered through hundreds of years of experience, and it can be incorporated into our daily lives. The various practices described in this book have their roots in these teachings. They deal with how we can relieve this distress of negative past impressions and clear out the storehouse embedded deep within; how to create positive impressions or affirmations, and how to direct our lives in the most creative and spontaneous way. ICR is therefore far more than just a practice, it is actually an attitude, a state of mind, and a way of being.

3

The Relaxed Mind

After meeting in America and being married in England, Debbie and I went on to stay in India, Nepal, then Australia and New Zealand. We did this in order to spend time in monasteries and ashrams, to be with our teachers and practise meditation, as well as to travel. We found tremendous spiritual nourishment in this way but we also found, outside of monastery life, a consistent and mundane routine of human existence. Here we were, far from our respective homelands, but there was little tangible difference! Instead there was a familiar commonality embedded in all the various cultures we visited.

Everywhere we noticed that people would get up in the morning, see to their toilet, have breakfast, go to work, come home and watch television. It was a pattern that, although repetitious, provided shelter from the fear of self-confrontation. We found this even in India, which I had first visited in 1968. At that time it had seemed like being on another planet, as it was so different from the Western culture that I was used to. But by 1986 it was commonplace to see colour televisions everywhere. I could hardly believe that in this poverty-stricken country such a pastime could be tolerated. But, as everywhere else, watching TV filled the gap of emptiness. The need to be comfortable, to enjoy oneself and be entertained, affects everyone; the dress, the religious beliefs and the customs may vary, but the underlying drive is the same. I remember being in a small village in the Himalayan foothills and seeing a young boy standing in front of the mud hut he apparently lived in. The clothes he wore were shabby, and he was so thin that I wondered what he got to eat. But he was holding a large ghetto-blaster.

Seeking a way out

In our apprehension and distress it is natural to look for means to escape, for ways to be free of this predicament. In so doing we create a web of protection around ourselves. We hide from the world in our own familiar space, never allowing in anything that threatens this pattern. We hold on to our thoughts and ideas, unwilling to change them, because in this way we feel we have some security. No one wants to be distressed – it is confining, like being in a cage. And although we may feel superficially as if we are not stressed and that everything is fine, just beneath the surface we are full of tension, reflected when we bite our nails, play with our hair, tap our feet or pace up and down. Perhaps we talk or eat compulsively, or are worried that someone is going to break into our homes. Or we hold on to feelings of how it used to be, and how we wish it would be.

A scattered mind is easily roused to irritation and anger. Yet whatever it is that we are disturbed about in others is often what is actually what we need to look at in ourselves. As Confucius said, 'When we see men of a contrary character, we should turn inward and examine ourselves.' We get stuck because we freeze and panic, life becomes overwhelming, we get stressed and then blame it on external situations. When this happens, all the negativity pertaining to that particular event arises in our minds. We become irrational and over-react, and the situation may even become unbearable.

A relaxed mind responds differently: it is reasonable and freely spontaneous. It acknowledges that we all have needs that we want to be met, but it also knows that if those needs cannot be met then that too is fine. The relaxed mind does not get caught up in analyzing details, but sees beyond the immediate situation to a state of balance. When we have this attitude our lives become workable rather than overwhelming.

Our natural state is one of freedom, but it is as if we somehow lost our way and now can't find the directions. Just as a child acts with a complete naturalness and spontaneity, so also as adults we possess that freedom, but we have become inhibited. In order for us to be dis-eased there must have been a time when we were at ease. Now we actually have to work hard to regain that balance, one that is naturally ours.

Restoring that original balance is not easy unless we are willing to move out of our habitual patterns and see the world, our world, with an open mind. As the philosopher William James said, 'Genius means little more than the faculty of perceiving in an unhabitual way.' But although stress is a major issue in our lives that affects our health, relationships, families and work, and we really do want to relax, we still don't give it enough thought or consideration; we just assume that is the way we are and leave it at that. Being creatures of habit, we believe that we are not the relaxed type and don't put any effort into understanding ourselves further. Our habit patterns are very strong motivators, influencing our behaviour and activities. We become absorbed in them, even though we know they damage both ourselves and others. And they are not easy to break: we become helpless when confronted with the reality of our own behaviour. These repetitive patterns are the activity of a mind affected by inner stress. It is by not being aware of the nature of a quiet and relaxed mind that we perpetuate such mindless activities.

This inner peace is ours to experience if we wish. However, we too often breeze through life in a semi-conscious state, missing the true joys because we are unable to relax and bring meaning to our otherwise hectic lifestyles. Let us not forget that life can be simple and wonderful; may we appreciate that we have eyes and can see the vibrant colours of life, have ears that can hear the sweet sounds, and that we have a body that allows us to experience it all. May we appreciate the earth below our feet, the green grass, the smell of the soil, the trees and the sky above us; the marvel of the birds flying over our heads and the infinite magic of each precious moment. There is dignity with which we can live in this world and be a witness to the pulsation of this wonderful organic process, where we can see the ordinary as extraordinary.

Discovering confidence

A mind that is at ease is a confident mind, secure in itself. It is free and able to make important decisions, because it is fully in the present moment. A relaxed mind is a storehouse of creativity, healthy and productive, rich with new ideas. A relaxed mind sees the rising sun and all its potential, giving warmth and protection, whereas a stressed mind sees the setting sun, and is cloudy and stormy. We have the option at any time to be in chaos or to be free. A relaxed mind sees that life is a challenge and meets it with dignity and fearlessness, while a stressed mind is heavy and sees life as a burden. The choice is ours.

It is not unusual for us to wonder if this life is meaningless when we look at the world and see so much pain and suffering. When a loved one dies, everything seems to become so senseless. Do we just die and be done with it, or is there something more to it that maybe we don't know? How can we go further in our understanding so that these doubts and questions can be resolved?

When first probing in this way we need to ask: Is my mind relaxed? Am I stressed and uptight, or can I be peaceful? Am I able to see things the way they really are? Am I contributing to this world, or am I just being a parasite? Am I happy? Am I doing what I really want to do? Am I discovering my own true worth? Do I feel like a full human being? Our own state is constantly influencing that of the greater whole; what we are feeling in ourselves will colour the way we see the world around us. But true progress is not really possible unless our feet are firmly on the ground and we are in touch with our reality. When we are relaxed and our minds can be quiet and peaceful, then that peace becomes dynamic and we have a stronger foundation. Then we can go deeper and discover more, and soon we are answering our own questions. For when we are at peace within, we are at peace with our world.

What about drugs?

In the sixties people began experimenting with mind-expanding drugs as a means to address many of these thoughts. Slogans like 'Tune in, drop out' became a part of our language. These were sincere people who wanted to be free, who experienced a great deal of expansion and joy that was far beyond ordinary understanding and perception. It was as they called it, 'far out'. But it proved to be a temporary type of high because it altered perception and tended to be ungrounded in daily reality. The experience was also chemically induced and therefore impermanent. However, the energy of the sixties should not be overlooked as unimportant, for it was a starting point; it made us aware that there was much to learn and understand about ourselves and the depth of human potential, among other things.

The main difficulty with the mind-expanding drugs is that the glimpse of 'samadhi' or ecstasy that can be experienced is comparable to a bullet being shot into the highest realms. We can get there, but without any conscious knowledge of how that happened, and therefore how to do it without the drug. It is also difficult to return and integrate such an experience into ordinary daily life. Our understanding of reality has changed, but knowing how to put that change into perspective is sometimes unclear. The experience can then fade without any real clarity or understanding of what actually took place, although a sense of something profound having happened may remain and motivate more searching. A further delusion that occurs is that those using the drugs think they have discovered the truth, but sooner or later they are yet again caught up in mental chaos and ego games. Life has been said to be like a dream, and so drugs are like a dream in a dream. Often after using drugs it is necessary to go through a period of cleansing as the mind may have become fragmented. We need time to sort things out in our lives and re-evaluate our priorities. I remember Swami Satchidananda saying, 'If LSD can make you a saint, then you should be able to take a pill to be a doctor, a lawyer, a politician or an engineer. For it is much harder to become a saint than anything else'. Drugs played an important role, but they did not provide a long-lasting answer. The Sixties were the beginning of a renaissance of consciousness, but it was immature. Now that we are entering into the Nineties many of the purer ideals of those times can manifest, but with greater understanding.

What is true relaxation?

True relaxation is a different ballgame. It is not a question of superimposing one stressful situation (like watching the news) on another (our already excessively worried and frustrated minds), but is a practical matter that works with both the body and the mind. It involves discovering a quietness of mind in which we can begin to see all the different ways we create stress, all the various means we use to keep the avoidance of self-confrontation alive, and it gives us the strength to let these go. There are specific mental exercises and relaxation techniques that we can practise, just as there are various stretching and breathing exercises that are helpful to ease the effects of physical stress. For instance, the system of hatha yoga is based on relieving the tensions in the body and mind, oxygenating the blood and brain, and purifying the nerves, as well as regulating the various organs. It is a beautiful, ancient system that was derived from yogis who lived in seclusion and austerity in the forests, seeing life as an organic dance of animals and nature. But no matter what practices we do, the important point is that true relaxation can bring about a level of peace and harmony in our lives that is completely out of our reach when we are stressed.

The 'relaxation response' refers to a state of deep psychological and physiological rest which affects every part of our nervous system, metabolism, controlling mechanisms and immune system. Our blood pressure is lowered and the heartbeat slows down; levels of stress hormones, particularly cortisone and adrenalin, are decreased; sympathetic and automatic nervous activities are decreased; muscle tension releases. At the same time, the capacity to concentrate is increased; efficiency and clarity are increased. The body's entire regenerative system is stimulated so that healing can occur, as well as the development of a greater resistance to the effects of future stress. Our sense of well-being is immediately increased, and this grows with practice.

Relaxation is an ongoing process, not a one-time shot. As we develop the process we are able to integrate deep relaxation into our lives. This involves having the right attitude and motivation, and an understanding of personal limits. It is a matter of recognizing our habits, our neuroses, our strong and weak points, and then learning how to deal with them in a non-judgmental way to bring about resolution. It means being willing to take time out in order to go within. However, it is not easy, particularly because of social and peer pressure. Due to the way we relate to ourselves and to each other in both daily life and society there is little space if we choose to change the basis of our lives. If we come to greet the world with an open heart, with compassion and love, we can often be regarded with suspicion – others do not trust our motives. We may be thought of as having hidden reasons for being so quiet or so nice. It takes strength and conviction to be open in this way.

Self-delusion and the ego

Ultimately our purpose in life is to encourage our own evolution and growth in a positive and constructive direction. This human birth is the only means we have through which we can realize our true nature and, as the Eastern religions teach, free ourselves from the cycle of birth and rebirth. Yet life as we know it seems a long way away from what the Eastern teachings are talking about. Life seems far too full of pain, problems and suffering to be able to relate to or realize such higher truths. As mentioned earlier, we are predominantly preoccupied with self-centred activities and the preservation of our egos – hence our belief in someone who is not.

The ego is the 'I', the 'false self', all the me's and my's that create separation, greed and selfishness and cause so much resistance and distress. Our lives are structured in such a way that we are slaves to our egos; we have a compulsive need to be serving this self-proclaimed master at all times. With the use of the senses the ego is constantly giving commands: through the eyes when it sees something it must have, through the tongue when it wants to taste something, and through the mind when it must control something. This ego makes demands on us by its need for more; it thrives on wanting more materially or on having more power over others. How often have we seen someone who is taking all the attention, is boastful and tries to be one-up on others. Then people say, 'He's on an ego trip', because he has no thoughts for anyone else but is only looking out for himself. In its need to sustain itself, the ego is relentless.

The four noble truths

However, the first teaching of the Buddha was that of the Four Noble Truths, and here we find that our unhappy human situation is exactly the ground from which growth can take place. For the ego is really a false sense of who we think we are. It is a master who exists only as an illusion. It stands in the way of allowing us to see things in the light of truth because it is biased by its self-centredness. It is this ego that is so often damaging; it particularly prevents us from being generous and compassionate. And it wants to keep us from being relaxed, for when we deeply relax we see this ego for what it really is and begin to go beyond its demands to a more selfless and free space.

The first Noble Truth describes the state of pain, the illusion and ignorance; it explains how the world is full of difficulties and suffering, that nowhere on the mundane, relative, level will we find a freedom from these states, for they are the very nature of human existence. How well most of us know this to be true!

The second Noble Truth describes the cause of this suffering as being that of our ego-centred desires: our desire that life should be different, our greed for more, our inability to accept things as they are. It is our own desire that causes suffering; our constant searching for happiness and our attachment to the physical world. We spend time either going after what we want, or trying to avoid what we do not want. It is an endless cycle.

The third Noble Truth says that there is a way out of this cycle of desire, that life does not have to be like this. Such a change implies that we must be prepared to release our desires, to see the ego for what it really is. For freedom from suffering means being free from compulsively wanting things; it is an acceptance and appreciation of how things are.

The fourth Noble Truth describes the way to freedom that the Buddha taught: that of learning relaxation, meditation, becoming generous, developing compassion and wisdom. All these qualities enable us to go beyond our selfishness and to become free of egotistical desire. This does not mean we have to become wandering monks – rather we can discover great joy and satisfaction in what we do have, and do not worry if we do not have; for we can discover the wealth and riches that already lie within. This wisdom is based on the teaching that all things are impermanent, and that nothing will last for ever no matter how hard we pray! If we deny this, then we just bring more suffering to ourselves, for the idea of permanence is an illusion. And if we can really accept this it brings great peace, for we become free of attachment.

Growing old gracefully

Each individual is on his or her own evolutionary journey. No two people are at the same place at the same time. We have all come to this world with our own things to work out. That is why people appear to be so different, all involved in their own processes. It is up to each one of us to learn how to work through and understand what we need, in order to go further on the path. It is not that we necessarily have to join in or become anything, but the teachings are there to give us insight and guidance. Teachers are beneficial because they are human beings who have worked on themselves and discovered the truths reflected in the teachings to be real and effective.

They are passing on their knowledge for the benefit of others who earnestly want to know. They see things in us that we may be blind to, and can encourage those things that help us grow. In our search for a better life free from stress, confusion and misery, we can understand that there is hope and that our lives can become not only manageable but also full of ease and clarity.

Because survival is one of the basic fundamental human activities and our concerns with it dominate our very existence, we naturally feel uncomfortable with the distress it can bring. Have you ever been to a nursing home and noticed the plight of the elderly in their struggle with the discomfort of old age? I know the subject is one we usually try to avoid because our society is based on living forever with the avoidance of old age and death. But keen observation can enable us to have a better understanding. For when we are awake within, then there is no real death: physical death is simply a transition, not an end. Usually, as we grow older, our minds are not relaxed; they are full of neurosis and deep fear of what lies ahead. We may become tense, angry at the world for what it has done to us, angry at our families for leaving us. We end up bitter and confused, wanting to die but also afraid of death.

One of Debbie's clients was a ninety-year-old woman who was not only very lazy about paying her bills but also very stubborn. Eventually Maggie's family had to take her chequebook away as she kept spending more money than she had and they were constantly bailing her out. They gave her plenty of money to live on, but Maggie fought and complained and was very angry about having had her 'independence' taken away, as she saw it. Debbie tried to explain to Maggie that her independence was intrinsic to her being, was inside her, not in her chequebook. It didn't matter who paid the bills, what mattered was the joy and happiness she could feel in being alive. But Maggie was too locked into her rigid thought patterns to be able to have this understanding. A case like this is a good example of how people may age physically, being seventy or eighty or even older, but their consciousness has become like that of a selfish child. They are engrossed only with themselves, unable to see beyond to the bigger picture, to see how irrelevant the material world really is.

Most of us grow old but we don't grow up. We don't mature – meaning we don't become wise, we are still ruled by what is labelled either right or wrong, we live with prejudiced views and limited understanding, and we haven't grasped what it is to be a full human being. The stressed mind is gross, often impenetrable, like a mirror that has accumulated a lot of dust. We have to take time to clean and polish it, because only then can we see our true reflection.

Firstly we can let go of the way we think things should be. We can stop blaming others and the world for the way we are; stop blaming ourselves for being incompetent when we fail or make mistakes; stop putting ourselves down for being stressed and thinking we will always be this way. And we can accept that we are capable of moving from a state of stress to one of relaxation, that we are able to change. For instance, do we get nervous or angry when events don't go as planned? Do we need to control things, or can we allow them to take their natural course? Are we manipulative or accepting? Can we forgive, or do we bear grudges and hold on to things? Are we confident within ourselves? Can we stay balanced? These are the things we need to look at honestly and work with, so we can become more tolerant and compassionate towards ourselves and others.

The effect of the relaxed mind

The breakthrough from stress to relaxation, to the relaxed mind, takes great positive initiative and brings enormous relief. When we make the transition from a lack of confidence or little faith in ourselves to self-confidence and inner knowledge, then we see the power of true relaxation. It creates the ability to see things as they really are. The stressed mind has no centre and lacks clarity, wisdom, self-assuredness and meaning; a relaxed mind sees meaning in all things. It is fresh and full of 'prana', the life force. Here there is movement and activity, whereas a stressed mind is static, lacks energy and is dull. A stressed mind is grey, a relaxed mind is clear and bright.

We tend to think that the opposite of stress is passivity, so all we need to do to have a relaxed mind is to become quiet and passive. But then we wonder how we will ever get anything done, and feel we will never be able to compete or achieve if we are so passive. So we believe that we need to be stressed in order to be motivated and activated. However, passivity need not be the opposite of stress. Rather we can discover a state in which we are totally effective and totally at ease with ourselves at the same time. We are then able to deal with life and all of its demands without becoming depleted; we have a natural resource within us that keeps us in a state of balance, relaxation and alertness. We may appear passive at times, but within us there is complete awareness of all things. We are both dynamic and relaxed.

Such awareness allows for a loving generosity to develop, freeing us of obstacles, we become trusting, content and at ease in situations. To give of ourselves for the sake of others, not because of what is in it for us, is natural generosity; to give what is worthwhile and to give it without attachment. This can be seen in the three traditional aspects of giving taught in the Buddhist scriptures: the giving of things, the giving of loving protection, and the giving of loving understanding. Yet how often are we giving in the hope or expectation that something will be given in return? Are we able to give freely and unconditionally? To see that inherent in the act of giving is joy? Generosity, loving kindness, compassion, faith and fearlessness are all human qualities, not superhuman ones. They are qualities that nurture a relaxed mind, a mind that is effervescent. This mind of ours is the most powerful instrument on earth. Positive thoughts in a relaxed mind can move mountains.

Ideally these positive characteristics of the relaxed mind form the foundation of our movement in life. But the world as we know it does not educate us or help us to develop such necessary qualities. The rules of life are the rules of the jungle, self-serving and often destructive. It may take a great hardship or upheaval for us to realize that we need to change, as we are products of habit and fear anything different. It can even take a whole lifetime to see the futility of our discontent! Nevertheless, a situation can occur to show us the necessary steps we must take to understand those things that are truly important and valuable.

The ability to respond

It is up to us, we are the masters of our own fate. When we take responsibility for ourselves, it can be wonderful. For responsibility is simply the 'ability to respond'; it is to be sensitive to ourselves and the world in which we live and to respond to this sensitivity. We can become fearless warriors, be brave and not afraid of who we are; we can go beyond fear rather than run away from it, becoming gentle and accepting in the process. To be a warrior is to be loving and kind in the midst of our pain and struggle; it means not being afraid to cry when something deeply moves us. When the mind is relaxed and peaceful it is spontaneous and strong – it is no longer subject to influence.

In the Vajrayana teachings of Tibetan Buddhism they say we can turn dirt into gold, or turn a negative situation into a positive one. This is the way in which we can deal with our whole lives. Instead of being the victim, we can learn how to change our experiences so they are not stressful but creative. Instead of panicking, we can accept what is happening and see what is needed in order to make it better. If someone insults us, then we recognize that it is probably caused by a painful state within themselves and we can have compassion for them, rather then cause more insult by taking it personally and responding with negativity. It is a great gift for us to learn: not to create pain in this world, for ourselves or anyone else. We can become self-imposed victims of our human condition, or we can develop wisdom and compassion.

Recently I went to see a friend who had just been told that he had terminal lung cancer. He already had AIDS and had believed he would live for three to five years. When he found out he also had lung cancer and was told he actually had only between one and three months to live, he was greatly relieved as now he could begin to prepare for his death. His mind was relaxed: he had accepted what most of us might dread, that this was the way it was. It was a great joy just to be with him.

I realized how, if we could live each moment this way, we could alleviate so much pain. I had never seen anyone so brave. Instead of exhibiting panic and distress he chose to be open, loving, and make friends with his death. To many of us this could be the most painful and stressful experience, but this friend took it as an opportunity to make peace with himself and his world.

We can live like this and not get caught up in the habitual patterns that keep us slaves to every difficulty that arises. Life is not easy – there is pain; but we can minimize it by accepting that pain and not giving it energy. We only get into more stress by holding on to the unpleasant and then desperately seeking the pleasant. We constantly repeat this process: running from what we can't bear, even though it follows us wherever we go, and running after pleasure that we never seem to get. But we can learn from those things that bring pain, as so often pain is saying; 'Hey, look at me, I have something to teach you', and pleasure is saying, 'You may have me for some time, but when I leave I bring pain'. For inherent in pleasure is a seed of pain and vice versa, as long as we are in the world of dualities.

We have the power to make the choice as to how our lives are and will be, by becoming free of our own limitations and personal issues. Life may not be like calm water but we can ride the tide and not be afraid to get our feet wet, to jump in even if we think the water is too cold. Did you ever notice how, when you are at the beach and think the water is too cold to enter, you dip your toe in and shiver? You know that your intention when you first came was to go for a swim, but now you are hesitating. Then you become brave and jump in and suddenly it is invigorating and refreshing and you are glad you took the initiative. So often we are reluctant to take that extra step, the one that shows us that our fears actually have no ground. We have the strength and the willpower to overcome our difficulties but we need to make a commitment to jump in, a commitment to ourselves that we will persevere and be warriors. Yesterday's horrors can be today's strengths; we learn from hardships – they make us stronger. By accepting things and seeing the way they are we can acknowledge and love ourselves in the midst of it all. If there is a strong enough commitment, if we are genuine in the way we feel and we have the will to grow, then we will attract those things that will help us to understand ourselves further.

As we relax, the inner stresses are released before they can affect us. This leads to a deeper state of balance where we are able to leave behind the small and narrow mind-set and mature into a more aware and grounded being. The releasing of these inner stresses results in the outer stresses being released. In this way our lives can begin to ease and change, as the real transformation is coming from within. Can we let go of our normal reaction to stress and also let go of the excitement when the event is over? Can we let go of our tension enough to be able to relax deeply, then emerge from that relaxed state into full awareness when the situation demands? If so, then we are able to deal with life in a fully mature way, with awareness and sensitivity.

The distressed mind creates, fear, anger, loneliness, greed and ignorance. The relaxed mind is one that is fearless, generous and understanding. It is a mature mind, one that is able to love, to be compassionate, selfless and tender-hearted. A relaxed mind is not afraid of any darkness that may lie within, for the strength of self-knowledge is the greatest strength there is.

For the mind to exist it needs to cling to something. It is like the flame on a log: without the log there is no flame. So we believe that without stress, or without entertainment, we are nothing. When we relax we soothe that disquiet and discover that beneath all the confusion our nature is innately calm and tranquil, with a basic sanity which can be experienced very deeply. We begin to dissolve the ego by consciously releasing neurotic patterns and habits that promote this self image, that promote the stress of self, thereby cleansing the mind. The mind can then be freed of limitations, and the ego loses its hold; we can become creative and joyful, we are at peace with ourselves.

4

Inner Conscious Relaxation

W e have discussed our purpose for being here in this life, and the preciousness of this human birth as a means to realizing our true nature. We have seen how the ups and downs that we go through are there so we may learn the lessons that can then help us become stronger, wiser and happier human beings. Each fleeting moment is an opportunity for growth and discovery. We have looked at whether our lives are primarily an accumulation of possessions and power, or a journey within; whether our purpose is to gratify the ego, or to understand the joy of selflessness and giving. We recognize that we are all different, with varying needs, wants and expectations, and that life is a process of personal growth and evolution. Each one of us has a purpose for being here as long as we are alive, even if we are unaware of what that purpose may be.

We are also aware that there is stress in life, some of which is challenging while some of it leads to distress. We cannot hide from stress as it accumulates in our bodies and our minds, but we often accept being in a stressful state without doing anything about that state until it becomes unmanageable. We know that all we need to do is relax, but this is easily misunderstood; we think that relaxation can be accomplished by indulging in simple and mindless activities. At times this is necessary. But relaxation as we know it is often an escape from our ability to cope in a world of conflicting ideas, family pressures, beliefs and prejudices, rather than an acceptance of life as it is. Acceptance does not mean we have to agree with how things are, but it does mean that we are making peace with our world. Nowadays we are faced with more mental illness, drug problems and widespread unhappiness than we are willing to admit. We add each day to the list of disappointments, yet we are not minimizing the problem. We look in laboratories for answers when we need to be looking directly into our own selves. If we truly want to be at ease and release stress, we need to recognize it and be willing to do something about it.

The degrees of confusion we all experience may be different, but the truth is the same. The traditional teachings repeatedly tell us how the more we give of ourselves the greater will be our joy. But how is it possible to give if we are in a needy state? We know how to remove ourselves from the dangers in the world, but when our craving mind and senses are reaching out for gratification can we control these urges? The impressions that are buried in the subconscious and unconscious mind control our conscious behaviour, just as the way we are raised and the effect of the environment that we are raised in contribute to the way our lives are formed. If we are always drawn outwardly, if our mind is always engaged in some form of activity, it is very difficult to tap that space within that is nourishing and fulfilling.

What can ICR do?

In ICR we can consciously release these subconscious and unconscious impressions and free ourselves of the habitual patterns that control our lives. Through training the subconscious mind to relax, the conscious mind too, will relax. The process has to begin at home. Inner Conscious Relaxation is one method that begins the process of understanding how we can work with fear, confusion and stress. If we can learn to withdraw our consciousness from distraction, then there is a greater ease and simplicity. Just as we care for our material possessions, we can learn how to care for our greatest possession of all: our own being. That is why ICR is so important, it makes the journey of going within possible. The practice does not give us realization, but it does create the environment in which awakening and realization can take place. So the process of withdrawal is one of going from the gross to the sublime, and as we relax our consciousness becomes ever more subtle.

In our search for self-understanding we may have tried to sit for long periods of time in meditation. But when we sit for meditation and our minds drift and the tension is still there, then we may get frustrated and bored. We even feel we are not developing insight, that we are wasting our time, and we stop practising. When this happens the body and the mind become obstacles. It requires discipline and time to feel good about our practice. We jump the gun and expect this body and mind, that has been involved with endless dramas, to suddenly obey by being calm and quiet. Of all the things we do in life probably the most difficult is to sit still, for even if we have developed a good sitting posture our minds will create distraction. How rare it is for a person to sit perfectly still for any length of time! Our minds are easily side-tracked. So let us first learn to lie on the ground on a blanket or mat, or to sit in a chair, and become at ease with ourselves.

In having learnt how meditation leads to states of joy and ecstasy, we may have neglected to learn what precedes this. When we are a child we begin by crawling; then we stand up and fall before we learn to walk; when we are sure-footed we can finally run. It all takes time. The same is needed when learning about going within. Before we can sit and comfortably practise meditation we need to learn how to relax the mind, to withdraw and separate it from external distractions. Meditation can be a natural and spontaneous activity, as when we walk in a garden or on the beach and suddenly everything drops away and the mind is still and at peace. A moment when there is no time; there is a knowing without words. But in other situations we are locked into confusion and limitation and it is at these times that we can use help. When we withdraw the mind through deep relaxation it becomes more powerful and focused. Then we are able to practise concentration and meditation with greater ease. Until we learn how to withdraw the mind and senses to go inward, it is difficult for our consciousness to evolve. ICR is a simple and easy way to learn how to work with the mind. It is a method that teaches us how to be centred and go inwards; it is a joyful journey. The space of relaxation that we enter is a fertile field of infinite potential which enables us to discover the safety and strength within us.

The practice of ICR

I first learnt the practice of ICR from Paramahamsa Satyananda. I practised it with the other students in classes, but he also trained me when we were alone. He would guide me into a state of deep relaxation and while I was in that state he would give me instruction. It was an opportunity not only to receive his teachings but also to learn a completely different method of relaxation from any I had known before. It was enjoyable because I could lie on the ground with a blanket or mat beneath me and a pillow under my head and be comfortable. It wasn't necessary to sit upright and be concerned with having a straight back – it was a new way to practise that anyone could do, as the initial struggle of maintaining a correct posture was bypassed.

Before I went to India I had thought that sleep or sensory diversion were the ways to relax, but now I was discovering that this was not so. Here I was learning a traditional method derived from the tantras, the ancient Indian scriptures, that enabled me to relax consciously, and now I was learning that in order to relax we are to remain aware. I was fascinated when I saw that the activities people normally think of as relaxing actually cause more tension.

After thoroughly learning this technique I knew it would be helpful for others to learn how to relax with conscious awareness, without having to go to India or join a group or organization. I have taught ICR to a schoolteacher who then taught it to his pupils. He saw their performance greatly improve as they become more spontaneous, as their memory expanded and their energy level became enhanced. I've also taught it in prison to the inmates, most of whom were depressed and confused. Each week more of them came to the classes, saying that as they became more relaxed and at ease in themselves it was easier to deal with their imprisonment. I've used it with people recovering from surgery, with parents, with pregnant women and with the elderly, as much as I have with those coming home after a day of stressful work. It is especially helpful in dealing with insomnia, if practised just before going to bed.

Inner Conscious Relaxation is a Western interpretation and understanding of the Eastern teachings related to the workings of the mind. It is a practical way of dealing with the confusion, stress and frustration we all suffer from. It enables us to transcend the patterns and reactions of the limited mind. ICR is a method we can follow by ourselves, without the need to go to someone else to do it for us. It offers an easy way to go within ourselves, because the instructions are simple to follow. There is no struggling with the mind to try to stay in one place; it is a moving, flowing inward journey. Although seen as a foreign adventure to the average Western mind, going within is an opportunity to enjoy whole new vistas of experience and consciousness.

Usually, when trying to relax, the mind drifts and it is difficult to focus. So before we turn our minds inward it is important to learn how to be at ease with ourselves, so that step-by-step the distractions are removed. Then we can proceed to more advanced stages such as meditation and samadhi. It is not that we make something happen; but as we train the mind we create the possibility, the environment, for changes to take place. From our original state of ease we have created dis-ease; now we are moving towards a state of ease again. Actually to isolate our consciousness as we do in ICR, by withdrawing the senses and mind from the normal distractions, is an entirely different way of perceiving reality from the one we are used to. ICR is direct. It is soothing to the body and mind and represents the beginning of a new and wonderful experience that goes a great deal deeper than the intellect. The journey within is a very personal and healing experience.

The nature of the mind is to cling. The mind cannot exist

on its own and so it takes the form of an object, thought or external experience to identify with; our likes and dislikes influence the place where our mind is at each particular moment. If we are in a class or listening to a lecture, as we are listening we are also thinking; our minds are in the past or the future, and we are not fully present in the now. Our consciousness is connected to other issues, hence our receptivity is less. The information is not received into the brain because it is crowded, and there is so much distraction that no new impressions can be made. But when we can withdraw the mind from the external objects then we have the opportunity to improve our memory, deepen our knowledge and release our creativity. In this way our whole being becomes free to go through a powerful transformation.

In this practice we are therefore able to create the changes within us that will benefit the whole of our personality. Just as we can rearrange the house we live in to make it correspond to our lifestyle, so we can make a positive difference in the internal structure of our being. Instead of being ruled by our impulses and acting out some unknown feeling within, we can take charge by consciously 'cleaning house', entering the various chambers of our minds and rearranging the furniture, creating the environment anew.

When we sleep, the problems of our lives are still going on in our minds – sleep does not necessarily release tension on the inner levels. Those tensions can, however, be released in practices like ICR, as we need to reach the unconscious levels to relax truly. If we go to sleep at night after practising ICR we will be deeply at ease – we can really appreciate a night's sleep without the habitual disturbances we are used to. What we achieve in one hour of ICR is the same as four hours of regular sleep. That is why so many of the great teachers appear to be dynamos with superhuman energy!

Making friends with ourselves

As we understand the development of ICR we begin to realize that it is a process of making friends with ourselves. It is a joyous breakthrough to reach this relationship, and it goes through many stages; it is a marriage of the body and mind, a willingness to accept that whatever comes up in the relationship is all right. A softness and gentleness, a kindness, as well as a deep respect, are awakened. Decisions are made, based not on dependence on others, but by listening to our own needs. I remember the first time I decided to get my own flat. Before that I had lived with friends and was secure in the knowledge that I had others around me and wasn't alone. It was a big move getting my own home and being responsible – maybe I would be lonely? But I met the chance to be alone with great enthusiasm and it stands out in my mind as one of the first true steps I took towards what seemed like freedom. We are all alone, we are all refugees on this planet. Each step we take by ourselves in unfolding this great mystery of life is an enormous challenge. The beginning of freedom is a willingness to look at ourselves and accept what we see, no matter what we may or may not like.

It is not easy to be friends with ourselves in this way, for our conditioning is much stronger than we are aware of: we have to find the root and start to dig it out. Making friends with ourselves takes conscious effort; it is a continuous process that we are confronted with throughout our whole lives, because when we see ourselves we do not always like what we find. We have to have compassion and loving forgiveness for ourselves. As we begin to understand the human mind we see that each individual, in their own time, is facing their own issues. And as we accept ourselves we can accept others. It is not what others do to us that is the issue, it is our own understanding of ourselves that is important.

Eastern religions often refer to this world we live in as being a sleep or a dream; they say that when we realize our true nature then we will see this world as if it were not real. When we are asleep to our higher Self the dream, this life, seems quite real. Just as when we are asleep at night, in the dream state we are not aware of anything but the dream. We think of the dream as real. When we wake up in the morning we realize we were only dreaming. In the same way we think we see daily life as being quite real, yet if we look closely it does have a dreamlike quality. And when we awake to our higher Self, then that is the only reality. As it is written in Shankara

Archarya's *Atma Bodha**, 'The world of birth and rebirth is like a dream, full of desires and hates; in its own time it shines as real, but on waking it becomes unreal.'

During the practice of ICR we are neither asleep nor are we aware of things outside of us. Our faculties are functioning, the intellect and the discriminating ability are there, but the focus is on the movement of consciousness through the various parts of the body. Our awareness is on the breath going in and out, the awareness that we are lying on the ground, and the process of letting go as we sink into the carpet or floor, going deeper and deeper. In this way the subconscious and unconscious mind begin to relax and the impressions that were locked inside them start to be released.

These are the blocks and obstacles that are embedded in the deepest parts of our minds, the things that we know happened to us but we cannot consciously recall or bring to the surface. As we go deeper into the relaxation it can become quite dynamic and we may discover a sort of pandora's box, an accumulation of our hidden issues. As long as we maintain the visualization during ICR, these issues will not disturb us. We are going to the root of our doubts and confusions and releasing them at that deeper level. Our built-up anxieties, frustrations and disappointments may stay hidden unless we can gain a true understanding of how to remove them.

As we get to know ourselves, the lessons change and we realize that no one can harm us, that nothing happens to us unless that problem is already within us. In learning how to cut through the confusion we find that beneath all the suppression is pure conscious energy, rich in vitality, beauty and light. It is like being in a dark tunnel: as we pass through it there is a moment when it feels endless, when we think we might not make it, then suddenly we see the light of day. So although our minds are full of all sorts of neurosis, caught in the duality of success and failure, attraction and repulsion, there is the possibility to heal, to go to that place within that is beyond the duality. That is where the creativity, oneness and fertile ground of transformation takes place. There within us

---

* The teachings of one of India's foremost religious scholars.

is where we can experience the freedom and the joy and we can initiate true change.

ICR is a state of deep relaxation, but it goes deeper than what we think of as relaxation as we are going beyond the conscious mind. This is a feeling of being completely at ease with ourselves. When we deal with the mind we are working with an immense powerhouse of energy. In ICR we begin to gently focus that energy towards one point. Throughout the ages different techniques that lead to this state of relaxation have been developed in the various traditional teachings. These methods may be fairly similar to ICR as relaxation is, after all, a state of great simplicity: one of letting go and withdrawing.

The roots of ICR

The practice of Inner Conscious Relaxation is a contemporary definition (and therefore more accessible and easily understood) of the practice of Yoga Nidra, which developed from the yoga teachings originating in India. The ancient yogis spent their lives unfolding the mysteries of consciousness. They were the natural scientists who, through personal experience, brought forth the wisdom of the Self. Because we normally depend on the information from our intellect and senses, the mind is weak. But once we open the doors of the deeper mind, the superconscious, then we are at the root of creativity. Yoga Nidra literally means union and sleep, or a state that looks like sleep but is actually a conscious union of all the different aspects of our being, a state between sleep and wakefulness which is neither of these. This deep level of union gives rise to dynamic peace.

ICR is a form of Pratyahara, or withdrawal of the senses. Pratyahara is described in detail by Patanjali, the 'grandfather' of yoga, who lived over two thousand years ago. Patanjali divided the raja yoga teachings into eight stages that, step-by-step, deal with attitude, social and personal ethics, physical postures and breathing exercises for stimulating health and energy; and pratyahara, concentration and meditation for calming and training the mind leading to self-realization. In this way the raja yoga teachings offer a complete guide to living a saner and gentler life.

The basis of ICR practice

In the practice of ICR, through listening to the guiding voice (this may be a teacher or a friend, or an ICR tape is available from Element Books) we do not lose conscious awareness. When we know the practice we can do it on our own, following our own inner guiding voice. Gradually all other senses are withdrawn. By maintaining awareness we can consciously relax the body far more deeply than if we were asleep. In this state even self-awareness can dissolve and the mind enters into total relaxation. There is no need to try to concentrate or to follow every word the guiding voice says. It is more important simply to be aware of whatever is happening, maintaining an unbroken stream of consciousness. We may even start dreaming or seeing different pictures in the mind and stop hearing the guiding voice. This happens when the subconscious is coming to the forefront and releasing energy that is stored there. As this experience passes, our awareness naturally comes back to the guiding voice, without any effort.

Throughout the practice different visualizations and images are used to focus our attention as the samskaras are released, enhancing our level of relaxation and awareness. Consciousness is maintained at a hypnogogic state, the borderline between the conscious and the unconscious mind. This is kept aware by the guiding voice of the instructor. This voice is not manipulating or forcing a certain state, it is simply guiding us to discover our own intuitive inner knowledge and ability to let go. This is the very opposite of hypnosis and it is important to understand this difference. In hypnosis, the hypnotherapist will lead, direct and control the mind of the practitioner. Therefore, even though deep relaxation may be achieved, it is dependent on the therapist being there. The therapist maintains this power as the means to enable hypnosis to take place. In ICR each person is responsible for themselves. The guide is there simply to guide, with no sense of domination.

When we practise ICR, we start by rotating our awareness through the various parts of the body. More acceptance and recognition has been made in recent times concerning the connection between the mind and the body. Many alternative practitioners as well as scientific researchers using electrode stimuli have shown how each part of the body is directly connected to the part of the brain that also deals with feelings, sensations and thought patterns. In the ICR practice, awareness of each part of the body is achieved through a rotation of consciousness. This rotation is in a similar sequence as the order that the body can be found mapped in the brain. It is based on the system of Nyasa, literally meaning 'to take the mind to that point'. It is through the brain that we connect the body, mind and emotions into one harmonious unit. (In the brain the corresponding area is greatly out of proportion to the actual size of the part of the body involved. For instance, areas associated to the lips and fingers are far larger than their relative size in the physical body.) By rotating our consciousness in this way, from one part of the body to the next, we are systematically relaxing the brain. In this way there is a natural letting go and releasing of tension. As we familiarize ourselves with this particular sequence of relaxation, so we can 'tune in' to that state at any time, whether during the practice of ICR or not.

Further on in the practice we tune our awareness to sensations of heaviness and lightness, hot and cold, pain and pleasure. This works directly with all the parts of the brain that are responsible for balancing our inner and outer environment, our sensual experience in relation to our bodies and our world. It harmonizes and eases the two-way communication between our experience of, and response to, stimuli. As we become aware of the initial feeling of heaviness it is a message to the brain to let go completely, to 'sink into the ground'. In this way the physical body relaxes and the muscles and tendons are free to be at ease and to merge with the earth, to become one with the heavy density of the earth's energy. As we sink into this state, we are then directed to develop the experience of lightness, as if floating. This further relaxes the body and also begins to separate our consciousness from our physical experience.

This separation is developed by expressing the opposites of hot and cold. These two conditions are related to our emotions: we become hot with anger and passion, cold with hate and rage. So then we also experience the differences of pain and pleasure. Deep within our minds are all the impressions of pain, hurt, anger and injustice as well as those of joy, pleasure, happiness and love. These memories, our samskaras, are locked inside. By experiencing the opposites of pain and pleasure in a deeply relaxed state, we begin to be able to relax these feelings that are beyond our normal reach.

During this process we develop what is known as 'the witness response', where we are able to simply witness what is taking place, rather than being subjectively involved. As we become the witness we are no longer subject to ego-centred selfish desires, to becoming incited to anger or frustration when things don't go our way, or to over-riding elation when they do. We become free of these extremes, free to remain calm and at peace. In this way our mental and emotional faculties are balanced and freed of our ego-centred way of receiving the world.

We have seen how stress affects the body, so now we can see why relaxation on this deeper, conscious level should be so important. As we withdraw from the physical experience and relax the brain, so the alarm signals that emanate there are also able to be at peace. This liberates a great deal of energy, freed from constantly trying to balance and ease stress-related afflictions in the body. This freed energy can then be used to start healing and energizing those parts of our body and mind that have been weakened or damaged. Inner healing and resolution can thus take place.

5

Awakening the Resolve

In order to be free in life we need to make friends with ourselves, to accept who we are just as we are; then we can genuinely reach out to others, as ultimately others are simply an extension of ourselves. In this process we begin by loving: loving ourselves without conditions, without limitations, in respect of our basic humanness. We acknowledge that we are not perfect in everything we do, for surely we wouldn't be here if that were the case! We are here to learn about ourselves, about our world with all its good and bad qualities; to learn not to be judgmental, for that can be never-ending. Certainly there are some things we may prefer, and we have our own likes and dislikes, but what is meant here is something different, something more intrinsic to who we are. In order to communicate deeply with ourselves in this way we need to go beyond the dualities of life's opposites and experience our essence, the core of consciousness that is within us all.

We know we want to achieve something in life but are unsure of what it is; we flounder and make mistakes, which is a natural part of life. Hopefully we can pick ourselves up and continue with our journey, learning more as we proceed. We so badly want to succeed that we make all sorts of resolves to change our ways - to stop over-indulging, stop smoking, get up earlier, whatever it may be. We make all these resolutions but then find we don't have the inner strength to follow them through, even though we may try for a while. We get distracted and even forget.

However, there comes a time when we can make a resolve that can change our lives from the inside out, one that stays with us at all times. This resolve is one that is made during the practice of ICR, and it is special because it is made when the mind is in a state of dynamic and complete relaxation. When we are at ease in this way and the mind is clear and free from distractions, whatever we put into the mind at that time will take root. By making our resolve while we are relaxed we are opening ourselves to real change. A resolve in this sense is an affirmation, a declaration of a positive thought. It focuses on our purpose for being here and expresses our own highest aspirations. Through the resolve we find strength and guidance; putting it into action gives our lives real meaning. As the practice of ICR both begins and ends with making this resolve, it forms the very foundation of the practice. Using it effectively provides a powerful means both to release that which is holding us back, and to give us new direction and purpose with which to go forward.

The world we live in is our home and field of activity. What we do with our time and how we structure our lives is determined by many things: our past experiences, our family and friends, our society and environment. Generally our underlying concern is to make the most of this gift of life. It is rich and vital and we are a part of this wealth. But to express the inner warmth of love that is the fabric of it all we need to clearly direct our activities, mentally, emotionally and physically, towards such expression. The resolve can help us to do this, giving us the strength to be able to see past the many diversions. We can either embrace life as it is, or get caught in the web of discontent; we need to become aware of our limitations in order to become free. There is a tendency to deal with life almost as if it were a business, fearing to embrace it fully because we don't want to get hurt, or be seen to stumble. We dare not show our ignorance as it leaves us so vulnerable. We know how to do so many things like fixing a car, building a bridge or flying a plane, but we are not always able to love unconditionally, even though it is the only way to deal with the varied conditions we face, and to deal with them with greater acceptance and freedom.

In a way our very lives are a resolve, for they are a statement of who we are. We resolve to do something with ourselves while we are here, whatever that may be. Life is a process of growing, learning, changing and developing. It is an exploration of ideas and feelings, a sharing and a giving. Many of us spend our lives trying to get more and more, but actually there is nothing to get – rather it is a process of ungetting, of unfolding.

A statement of unity

A while ago I attended a conference called Unity in Yoga. Representives from all over the world, including the USSR, South America, Great Britain, the USA and India were there, as well as those of various faiths: Christian, Jewish, Hindu, Moslem, Sikh and American Indian. The message was that there are many paths, all leading to one truth. Swami Satchidananda pointed out that 'yoga' actually means 'unity', but that even within the many fields of yoga there are differences. The gathering and sharing was an expression and a resolve to understand that unity in the diversity. In other words, we may all have a different personal resolve but within each of us is the longing to come together and share what we know and how we feel, to go beyond the superficial differences of colour, class or creed.

So within this vast spectrum our needs vary accordingly. Each individual's resolve may be different from that of the next, but we can respect the needs and the lessons of each one of us. This great university of life will test us: sometimes we fail, at other times we succeed, but in the process of learning wisdom begins to emerge. As Swami Satchidananda says, 'The universe itself is a university. People come as students; they study and learn....When you understand the world, and realize your own true nature, you get the diploma.' We are all human, and can be both tender and strong; with the right attitude and the resolve to appreciate this precious life we can endure on our journey. We may fall sick, get stuck or become overwhelmed, but the resolve will keep us going when all else fails. With a resolve of unconditional love we can water this flower of life and liberate ourselves from limited consciousness.

Making our personal resolve

In formulating our resolve many different aspects of our personality can come to the foreground to be dealt with, most especially such issues as: What is our real purpose? What is our deepest desire in life? What do we really wish to achieve, beyond our materialistic fantasies? We may find that we don't know the answers to these questions because we are not in touch with our deeper aspirations. We have simply gone from one event to another without any great sense of purpose. Now that we are being confronted with choice we can actually choose our purpose, voice it clearly and create a new positive direction. Each one of us needs to find the resolve that is right for us. Some examples are:

'I am relaxing and I am healing.'
'I am an instrument of unconditional love.'
'I am awakening to the truth, for the sake of all beings.'
'I am causing no harm, to either myself or others.'
'I am finding the peace within that others may also know their peace.'
'My life is a service to all mankind.'
'I am realizing my true nature.'
'I am one with all beings.'

Did you ever wonder how five billion people could live on this planet and still survive? Isn't it extraordinary! And yet it's happening. Isn't that unconditional love from mother earth? We all live under this warm sun, receiving light, and the sun does not ask for thanks. We all breathe the same air, and the air just continues to give. The world we live in loves us unconditionally, and we so easily forget to appreciate this. Yet we can be free. We can be in prison behind bars and be free. And we can be in the free world and be enslaved. The resolve we make in our lives can facilitate this freedom. If the earth can so lovingly sustain us yet we cannot sustain ourselves, then it shows that there is a need for us to compromise our differences, to become flexible, to understand the unity in diversity. We can appreciate the differences as a joy to be shared, rather than giving energy to the ignorance and the separation it can incur.

The planet needs to heal as each one of us needs to heal, so that too can be a resolve. As we make our personal resolve it becomes clear that this strengthens the planetary resolve. We can pray for those who live in ignorance, who destroy each other, who destroy this planet. And we can put our energy into our resolve. If we make a resolve we do not really believe in – one that is purely intellectual, or one that is not a true reflection of our inner being – then we will not be committed to seeing that resolve ripen. So let us choose one that is meaningful to our lives.

Living the resolve

As we repeat the same resolve each time we practise ICR, so that resolve takes root in our unconscious mind and is able to grow there. This is why it is important that the resolve should be one we really believe in. Just as the old impressions may influence our behaviour in a dysfunctional way, so the resolve can start to influence our behaviour and actions to bring about transformation of a truly positive nature. If we are to encourage world peace we must first develop and experience our own peace each day, for the rest of our lives. It is not a one-day or even one-year process. We don't just change and it stays that way. There is no magic potion we can take so that everything becomes OK. But through sincere work and a willingness to be honest with ourselves we can develop greater insight and awakening. We can see things in a new light, expand our limited awareness and change our point of view.

Nothing is fixed, nothing is permanent; it is natural that we change and expand. But so many of us get stuck in our own smallness, in our narrow mind-set. We move a little, and then get stuck again. We want progress and then fail to instigate it.

We meet teachers of wisdom and become inspired, and then fall back into old patterns, letting our minds play tricks on us. Making an inner resolve is a reminder of our intent; it is fixed in the deepest part of our being. Then our lives can be motivated by that inherent power. The forces of ignorance are much too great to just relax and think that things can go on the way they are. Many unforeseen situations occur that we are not prepared for, so when we remember the resolve it brings that energy to life and we can cut through the limitations that are holding us back. The resolve can be a tremendous source of strength and inspiration.

When I was at the Unity in Yoga Conference, the Soviet delegates shared with us their resolve of bringing the understanding of unity to the USSR, by gathering people together in dialogue and practice. In this way we bring down the barriers that separate us, bringing us closer to ourselves and each other. The fears, doubts and ignorance that have been perpetuating on a global level are slowly breaking down. What a great joy to see so many changes! It is inspiring to see the commitment of people throughout the world who are living their resolve to encourage awakening, both individually and globally. As the barriers come down we become more aware of the spiritual renaissance that is happening, internally and externally. Let us not hold on to differences, but cherish the many ways and expressions of love that exist.

By putting the highest ideals first as our purpose, so the lower energies lose their power, enabling the higher ones to manifest within us. However, we are dealing with the ego! There is both a personal ego and a collective ego; there are many forms, for ego is simply the ignorance of separation. The personal ego is the I, mine, me. But there is also a Jewish ego, a Christian ego, a Buddhist ego, a black, white and yellow ego, and so on. The ego dissolves when we actually embody the truth that is within us all, a truth that is hidden by our own inability to go deeper within. This truth then enables us to see our world clearly, free from obscuration, without illusion or egotistic involvement.

We see things the way we do because we are growing and learning; as we change, so does our vision. Pain is there to point out that something needs our attention. We do not always know how to deal with pain, because it asks us to be honest – and that too is painful. Being quiet, asking for inner guidance and developing the resolve, are ways to deal with these confusing and painful experiences that life offers. When we make a resolve, all those issues resisting the resolve often arise; they may be difficult to bear, but they are our aid in reaching the fruition of the resolve. For instance, if we want to be peaceful then opposite circumstances may arise, for only when we can go above our dualistic nature is there real peace. As long as we are involved with relative consciousness there will be a need to learn how to discriminate, to apply discriminating wisdom. Often when we confront a situation that is giving us pain, if we look deeply, we see that it is the pain of the ego, that we are in a fixed, self-centred mind-set, and that in order to be free of the pain we have to let go of the ego. The pain will be there and rise up each time we don't expand our view to that of the greater whole. We use our resolve as a means to change. It is a commitment to ourselves to be flexible, to be spontaneous when at times we think we are unable to be, and to stay true to our ideals.

Power of the resolve

When we choose our resolve, it should be one that is meaningful to our whole lives. As a resolve is so powerful it is advisable to use it for the highest aspirations, it is a means to create a whole new direction in life. However, we may need to clear the smaller obstacles (like drug or alcohol abuse) before such transformation can fully manifest itself. So if necessary we may use the resolve for therapeutic reasons. Using the resolve to change our lives means that behaviour patterns like these will inevitably change too. The resolve is our means for this to happen, and its power should not be underestimated. The greater view will benefit all of our being and help remove any bad habits naturally.

It has been seen that people in prayer, creating positive thoughts of love on one side of the world, can help heal a sick person on the other side of the world. Thoughts are immensely powerful: they cause pain that can erupt in illness, and equally they can bring healing when positively focused. They determine the direction we go in. As we create a more positive lifestyle we begin to attract those situations that uplift and bring joyful results. As mature individuals, if we can bear insult and injury, then we can stay balanced and grow into the full person, the full potential of a human being that is our highest aspiration. Our resolve becomes the foundation from which we grow.

The resolve is a seed that facilitates positive motivation. When our energy is depleted by negative action, we lose ambition and vitality and spend too much time pondering useless frivolity. As the mind dissipates, we lack energy and purpose. This can happen so easily. Will I succeed? What will happen if I fail? As soon as we set out to do something all the fears arise, all the things that prevent the fruition of our purpose enter into the field of our mind to test us and our sincerity, to see if we have the fortitude to persevere. The power of the resolve charges our whole being at these times to carry on in the direction that best accomplishes our aim. The resolve made in ICR is being planted deeply in our minds and will thus bear fruit. The integration of the resolve will destroy the obstacles by the sheer strength of its presence. In being planted in the subconscious and the unconscious it affects our whole lives.

Many of us are aware of the importance of such positive thinking. The renaissance of consciousness is constantly reaching more individuals, and as we develop a selfless attitude and see the benefit of giving – making our lives a continuous flow of giving – then healing can take place, both individually and globally. Wholeness is a planetary issue. As we think of holistic living there can be no barriers. True holistic living is seeing the oneness, the unity in diversity. I am not saying we should all become the same, or that the world will become totally free. It doesn't happen that way. As Swami Satchidananda explains, 'Don't expect the whole world to be enlightened one day. It would be like walking into a Detroit automobile factory and seeing only finished cars! If the factory were full of finished cars, it would no longer be a factory: it would become a showroom.'

The earth is a place to learn and grow – it is our spiritual training ground or boot camp! We can improve our understanding by working with ourselves and our limitations, and the resolve is a key for us to use in releasing the negative patterns that hold us back from moving forward. It helps us find the way to expressing our higher ideals. The process of ICR is an ideal method to use, as the resolve within it is a statement that focuses our energies on the highest and helps us unfold our potential. With one-pointed awareness the resolve gathers the scattered energies of the mind to create what is most important for us as individuals, for the benefit of our evolution.

It is rare for most of us to know how to enter into the subtle dimensions of the mind, to go from the gross to the sublime. We usually get caught up in the fluctuations of the mind and ego and are unable to perceive the light of wisdom. When the resolve is planted in the relaxed mind, then the very nature of its power clears away that which prevents its fruition. The mind is an instrument, and a good practitioner can play a very beautiful tune with it. Deep within us is our own resolve. When we find what it is we should stay with it, for it can bear great fruit.

6

Dimensions of Consciousness

Our body and mind are our instruments, our vehicles for moving from one place or state of awareness to another. In this context it is possible to experience extraordinary levels of consciousness, for when we expand our minds we can become enriched by the vast wealth there is available. As the writer Oliver Wendell Holmes said, 'Man's mind, stretched to a new idea, never goes back to its original dimension.' Through practical means and self-enquiry we can begin to experience the wonders of this creative, intuitive human marvel, our treasure-house of joy. Beyond our thoughts and intellect is an ocean of consciousness that is vibrant, vital and more satisfying than any words can describe. As we carve away the layers of illusion the shining light of wisdom is revealed. Just as a diamond is hidden in rough raw stone, there is a jewel more beautiful than any known waiting to be discovered within us. Each positive action that is done with an open heart has the potential of bringing us in contact with this jewel, and as we move in the direction of its rays we feel it's luminosity and power. Nothing in life is more satisfying, more nourishing and more meaningful to our existence. For it is our own true Self!

If we already have it, then why do we need to do anything to realise it? This can seem illogical! However, we live in a world that is basically functioning on a materialistic level; we have a society that is entrapped into fulfilling external and egotistical needs and our minds are constantly drawn into this by our desires and our samskaras. Just as a lotus flower grows from a heap of mud, so we have our sticky, thick mud that hides the budding flower within. Our limitations, negative views, fears, repressions, doubts and confusions form our mud, and we become clinging and attached to these. But just as the lotus needs the mud from which to grow, so our mud is the very nourishment we can use for us to develop, expand and realize ourselves. In understanding, accepting and integrating this mud, rather than denying it, we can use it as a fertile ground from which our lotus can bloom.

Expanding the mind

Most of us were born in a certain area and then maybe moved to a new part of town or country. We grew out of the old neighbourhood and into new vistas. As we constantly move out of old places and societies, so in the process we expand our views. We expand each moment, each day and each year. For instance, we probably had certain belief systems that worked in the past but are not valid any more. We may have grown up believing that God was to be feared and we had better be good or else. But now we may believe or know that God is within us, and we want to be selfless because it feels right – it makes sense – rather than because we are fearful. We can expand with understanding, with love, and discriminate between that which is skilful and helps us, and that which is unskilful or holds us back.

The process of expanding the mind has seen many expressions of understanding and experience, such as in the sixties when it was assisted by mind-expanding drugs. This was a sincere wish for things to be divine. The truths that were uncovered were valid, but the means to interpret them are still being worked out. The dream of wholeness never left, and we are now in a period when barriers of all sorts, whether personal or political, are being removed. But that change first has to take place in the human mind. By working with ourselves and with the practices of ICR, through visualization and meditation, we can develop a means for penetrating into the vastness of consciousness. This is also called the superconscious. It is super because of its radiant, limitless, all-pervading joyful qualities. The wisdom and intelligence that we discover is not something we learn from outside but is revealed when we open up and become free within ourselves. It is when the veil of ignorance is removed.

As we expand we can become aware of the various energy patterns that are within us. Our consciousness moves between our will to live, the basic survival instinct, and our will to be realized, to go beyond the mundane. We have the potential to express all sorts of different personalities and human characteristics: sometimes we are like animals, at other times we are divine. The different levels of energies within us are often unconscious; strong drives and motivations influence us to behave according to how we feel and what we believe we want to achieve. As we get to know more about ourselves, we have the opportunity to direct our own reality. We can learn to act or respond rather than react to life. A reaction is a reflection of habitual behaviour patterns where little thought is involved. A response reflects sensitive, thoughtful expression – one based on a consideration of all the factors present, not just the subjective ones.

Our purpose here is not just to consume as much of this world as we can. Nor are we merely intellectual robots collecting information for the sake of inventing more technology, endlessly processing inanimate matter as if in itself there was wealth that could be intrinsic to discovering who we are. Invention has its place, the intellect may be necessary, but it too is an egocentric device. Being alive means investigating our nature on a more profound level, beyond the intellect and the grosser dimensions, to the essence. What we think of as extraordinary levels of consciousness are, when investigated, actually quite natural and inherent to who we are.

For thousands of years yogis and mystics have explored these vast regions of consciousness. They have expounded on the infinite, inexhaustible energy that lies dormant in each being. We may think of this wisdom as being far away from our own reality, or as not scientific enough to give it much attention or credence. It is easier to accept that something is real when we are looking at it in front of us and we can see it or feel it as tangible. It is not so easy when we are dealing with the more subtle realms. Although the seers speak about how the purpose of life is to find the inner path to enlightenment, we tend to ignore the message. We think the possibility to experience what they are saying is only for the few, and we do not believe we can do it too. For it is not easy to comprehend on our own, to go against the norm and create a path different from that which is walked by society as a whole. But what one human being has done, each human can do. At some point we become ready to give up the futility and conflict of a purely materialistic existence, and accept the possibility that we can remove this veil of ignorance through our own initiative. There are many names given to describe this infinite potential that we are all capable of experiencing – a state that so wonderfully defies the limited pleasure of external existence, and reveals the exquisite happiness that can be discovered within us. As we clear away the neurotic, petty and at times hopelessly clinging mud, all the inhibitions that limit us, then the glory of who we are can be known.

Seeing through the illusion

In order to understand that the happiness we seek is not outside of us, we have to revise our conceptual way of viewing life, the one which society has perpetuated. We spend our energy on conquering the physical world because most of us are wary of making our own way in the spiritual world. For here the territory appears uncharted. However, the wise men and the various scriptures remind us that we do have a means to salvation, and that we can discover this by looking to ourselves to find the teacher within. Through ignorance we have seen God as an external form, rather than seeing that we already have the answers ourselves. We make idols of our gurus and adopt their answers, instead of seeing that all they want is for us to find our own truth. We deify and make gods of others, while the god we are searching for is within us.

Much has been written in the Eastern scriptures, describing this physical plane of existence as maya* or illusion, but this description is often decried by Westerners as simply a way to keep people pacified in the poverty-stricken, technically under-developed nations. Corruption and power so easily dominate and distort the truth. So the fact that life may actually be an illusion is not considered by the rational Westerner. Yet this description of our existence is an apt and accurate one and applies as much to prosperous countries as it does to poor ones.

For the illusion is not only an illusion of having or not having, it is the illusion of believing that by having we will find happiness. When we don't have things, then we seek to have them because it appears that it will solve our problems and give us greater joy. If we have things we fear to lose them, because we think it will bring unhappiness, and so we spend all our time protecting what we do have. Material wealth is not the issue, for in itself it has no value. It is the importance we put on wealth that is disturbing, as it generates more greed, anger, violence, depression and hatred than any other aspect of our lives. Ultimately we realize that the only lasting joy is the joy that is free, that has no materialistic value at all. Our very confusion is actually the maya, the illusion in our mind that there is substance and meaning in that which is insubstantial, impermanent and therefore meaningless.

The tendency of the mind is to become absorbed in the senses as the mind itself has no ground of its own; it is like the flame on a candle that cannot exist without wax to burn. The mind is always clinging, reaching outwards for satisfaction through the senses which act like magnets, attracting and distracting at every opportunity. This constant need for stimulation is based on the fear of confronting our own emptiness. However, we are not just a bundle of flesh, blood and bones, nor are we just a mind that retains information and acts out of survival, lusting for impermanent material gratification. The inanimate things in life that we think we need and constantly want more of do have a purpose, for they enable us to be here. But do we possess them or do they

* Also veil of ignorance.

possess us? Have we lost the ability to discriminate, thus forfeiting the true for the superficial?

Entering the deeper states of consciousness

In going from the gross to the subtle levels of consciousness we unfold the many wonders of a true human being. As we quieten the mind, recognize our priorities and see things for what they really are, so our desires become less important. If everlasting peace is within us, and desire ultimately brings only pain, then let us explore the dimensions of consciousness that help remove some of the ignorance that pervades our limited, conditioned point of view. There are many ways we can unmask the layers of illusion. Each time we enter new dimensions of understanding, greater wisdom is revealed to us and there is deeper joy. We need to be fearless, cutting through our many levels of confusion, for truth to emerge. We can do this by living a life that expresses honesty and dignity, by being aware of the entrapment and power of the ego, by recognizing when we are being self-righteous or genuine, and by accepting it when we don't know. We work with transforming our limited mind to be able to realize the highest truth, and all that arises in the process of doing this is there to show us what is yet to be experienced.

We can use various methods such as ICR that help to focus the mind and enter into deeper states. As the more intuitive levels become accessible we may have experiences that are dreamlike, but we are not asleep. These are experiences from the subtler levels. To give an example, here is the story of a great yogi. One day, when he was a young seeker, his guru told him to meet him at the local park at noon the following day. The young man was prompt and waited for some time, but to his dismay his master never showed up. He was disappointed and left, wondering what the teaching in this situation could be. The next time he encountered his master he asked him why he had not come to meet him as planned. The master replied, 'You need to practise deeper meditation. I was there, but I was hiding behind the rays of the sun. Keep practising until you can see me!' This may seem exaggerated, but illustrates how subtle the mind is and the dimensions we have yet to experience. Most of us have only touched the surface of what there is to discover.

To know what is real we need to be able to recognize what is unreal, to be able to discriminate; to know truth we need to be truthful with ourselves and with others. Normally we play games - we play countless roles due to our over-indulgent egos. For instance, as we practise and learn more of the teachings we may get the notion that we have gained something, some special insight, and we begin to consolidate this. As we think we have made progress we get puffed up and believe we know and are more advanced than others, but this very attitude will hold us back! It is always helpful to have the attitude of being a beginner, which prevents our ego from becoming indulgent with our progress. That is why I say it is more a giving than a getting, because the process is an emptying, not a filling up. We have covered up the wisdom with our mud, our issues and conditioning, and now we are clearing away the ignorance. The enlightened state is already within us, and through practice, self-enquiry, purification and surrender it can be revealed. The depth of our insight into the dimensions and perceptions of consciousness is a result of our willingness to let go of the way we think life is or should be, and to open ourselves to the discovering of new possibilities and ways of being.

The witness

During the practice of ICR we simply become a witness with awareness, and in this way we can be free of judgement, analysis or rationalization. There is just awareness, free perception. If we were to be involved during the practice then the mind would be constantly interceding - there would be a conscious resistance to the images or experiences arising in the mind. By being detached we are able to release and move beyond the illusions and impressions in the mind, which become powerless. In this way we can become free of the habitual mind. This attitude of the witness is the ability to be objective even with ourselves, to be free from what we find, to see ourselves simply as we are, without subjective prejudices. This approach is not one that is cold and uncaring, it is joyfully filled with love and compassion, but it is without ego-centred passion. We can also develop this understanding in other aspects of our lives, for ICR is not just a practice, and such an attitude is a means to freedom.

Visualization

Within this detached and clear state of the witness we can use visualization as a means of contacting the impressions that are buried in the unconscious mind. Normally the way we can contact the unconscious is when we are dreaming. Dreams reveal the hidden patterns, and that is why we are so fascinated with what they are saying. In sleep we are able to release the conflicts and past experiences that have been suppressed or had their validity denied, and which have accumulated in the subconscious and the unconscious. But these accumulations can also be consciously activated in ICR through the use of visualization, which can bring forth these inner forces, for we use specific images to contact them and release their dominance over us. In the visualization part of ICR the symbols used are simply a catalyst to enable the unconscious to respond. Both recognition and release happen spontaneously as we consciously create the image, in accordance with the instructions of the practice.

If we are unable to visualize, then we can see the image as a thought. It is not necessary to try too hard for ICR is not a practice of concentration; rather it is unbroken conscious awareness that uses imagery and symbols to draw us into different levels of awareness. As we go deeper in our practice and are able to focus our minds directly, so we find the images coming more freely and clearly. This may take a while, so we simply allow the awareness to develop in its own time. When we are truly focused, the images will become brilliantly clear.

In this way, ICR enables us to make the connection between the unconscious and the waking state, thus developing a deeper level of communication within ourselves.

The collection of impression in the subconscious and unconscious is accessed and may be released into the conscious mind, but in such a way that there is full integration and awareness. Images, colours and sounds may spontaneously emerge, as can memories that are sometimes painful. By staying with the practice of visualization and not becoming involved with what arises, there is no ego involvement and the pain is easily released. Rather than being in a passive, forgetful state as we are after sleeping or dreaming, we are fully awake so the imagery can be brought into the conscious mind. And as the conscious and the unconscious mind come together we have access to a vast amount of information normally kept out of reach. We can thus become free of whatever is holding us back.

The five 'bodies'

In Western psychology when we refer to the dimensions of the mind we talk about the conscious, subconscious and unconscious. In the Eastern terminology they call them the gross, subtle and casual dimensions. Out of these three dimensions there are five 'bodies' or 'koshas', also known as sheaths, that define the whole of our being. This approach offers us a different and more expansive perspective to understanding the dimensions of our consciousness.

1. *The food body.* This comprises all the organs, tissues, skeleton and fluids, and all that is absorbed through our senses. It represents the grossest level, and is perceived as the physical body. It is the level of the conscious mind.

2. *The energy body.* This level consists of the main energy currents in the body such as our breathing, digestion, excretion, blood circulation, immune system, locomotion etc. It is our emotional and thinking energy, and is still at the level of the conscious mind.

3. *The mental body.* This is the energy that operates in the dimensions of the mind. It relates to all the mental processes such as deeper creativity, imagination and memory. This is the level of the subconscious mind.

4. *The psychic body.* This is where our consciousness is

experienced on the psychic plane, above the mental. It is the sphere of intuition, imagery and dreaming. This is also the subconscious mind.

5. *The bliss body*. This is where the mental impressions (samskaras), our unresolved issues, are buried. As they are released we reach the level of bliss beyond duality. This is the transcendental state. It is the level of the unconscious mind.

The chakras – levels of consciousness

We can use this understanding in further investigating the various dimensions of our being, as represented by the chakras, or levels of consciousness. One of the most powerful forms of visualization and imagery used in ICR is that of the chakra system, which symbolises man's awakening from the gross to the divine. Each chakra defines a different aspect of consciousness and is a unique way to see how we evolve in understanding. As discussed earlier, our true nature is that of being fully realized, so awakening these dimensions of consciousness is a natural part of our movement towards this realization.

The chakras are not physical but are centres of energy that can be located at various points in the spinal region. They bring together our physical, mental and emotional energies with our spiritual intent. The higher chakras are generally closed due to our preoccupation with the lower forces such as desire and power. It takes perseverance, practice and commitment to raise our consciousness and open ourselves to higher levels of being; it is a slow process of unfolding, and each one of us grows according to our own readiness. Our minds are multi-dimensional, and as we perceive the various chakras we gain greater insight and understanding of awakened consciousness. Moving from below the base of the spine up to the crown of the head, we move from the dense to the subtle levels of energy, from awareness of self to Self-awareness.

By withdrawing our senses we are able to connect with the energy and perception of each of the chakras, as they cannot normally be contacted directly by the senses. During the practice of ICR we use the different colours, forms and sounds associated with each chakra as a way to awaken their energy and to bring them into the conscious mind. We visualize each chakra as symbolized by a different lotus flower, in order to deepen the perception or consciousness that the chakra is connected to.

1. *Mooladhara.* The first three lower chakras are associated with human existence. This first chakra is connected to our animal nature, to our basic physical survival needs and primitive behaviour. At this level man is unconscious of himself, but as awakening takes place individual understanding and awareness arise. This is the realm of the body. It is the consciousness of materialistic desires and self-centred behaviour, where we find our deepest fears, guilt and paranoia. It is the root or foundation not only of the whole chakra system, but also of our existence. As described earlier, the lotus flower grows from the mud and this chakra represents that very deepest level of our own mud. For here also lies the coiled serpent, the kundalini, the dormant power that can rise up through the chakras to the highest experience of awakening, just like the lotus that grows upwards through the water to the sunlight.

Mooladhara is located inside the perineum in men, midway between the scrotum and the anus, half an inch inside; and in women in the cervix. It is represented by a four-petalled lotus flower in a deep red colour. The sound associated with this chakra is 'LAM', and the sense that of smell. The element symbolic of mooladhara is earth.

2. *Swadhisthana.* This second chakra goes from the awareness of survival to that of procreation and relationship. This brings into action desire, desire for more and clinging to desire; this in turn gives rise to the duality of pleasure and pain. This is the realm of the senses. It is enjoyment of the physical world in all its aspects. Swadhisthana is also the storehouse of the unconscious, of all the past impressions, experiences and events in our lives; it is the gathering-point of man's collective and ancestral energy. This energy is that which keeps us bound to physical existence, as represented by the urge for procreation.

Swadhisthana is located in the very base of the spine, in the area of the coccyx. It is symbolized by a six-petalled lotus flower that is orange-red in colour. The sound associated with this chakra is 'VAM', and the sense that of taste. The element symbolic of swadhisthana is water.

3. *Manipura*. This chakra is also known as the fire centre, for it awakens perception in the area of self-identity and ego, which includes the fiery energies of power and control. Those that function from this level want to dominate and are highly ambitious, with a desire for wealth and recognition. It is also the development of the more human qualities as opposed to the purely animal ones, for here emerges conscious discrimination and will. This is the realm of the mind. The use of will is normally associated with ego-centredness and achievement; but here also lies the will to enlightenment – the will to awaken, to go beyond the ego – and once awake this is an extremely powerful energy.

Manipura is located behind the navel on the spinal cord. It is represented by a ten-petalled bright yellow sunflower. The sound associated with manipura is 'RAM', and the sense that of sight. The element symbolic of manipura is fire.

4. *Anahata*. This fourth energy centre, which is also known as the heart chakra, moves our perception from the ego-centred state to that of the egoless state, from passion to compassion. Here we awaken the truly human awareness; from the body, senses and mind we now emerge into the higher realms. This is the development of unconditional love towards all of creation and leads us, through our devotion to the highest, to self-realization. It is the opening of the heart, a state of unity with all beings, free of egotistical desires or needs. The wise ones who have realized the highest of truths function through anahata, due to their compassion for all living beings. They see humanity struggling and confused, and through their compassion they bring understanding, meaning, acceptance and friendship.

When we experience the heart opening we may have tears of joy, heart tremors or overwhelming laughter; our bodies may tingle, our hair stand up or we may have goose pimples. We are overcome with surges of great flowing love. At first it may only be momentary, or it might last for some time. We will know when we have opened the heart centre as we will feel a constant flow of unconditional love.

Anahata is located in the spine directly behind the centre of the chest, behind the depression of the chest. It is symbolized by a twelve-petalled lotus flower that is blue in colour. The sound associated with this chakra is 'YAM', and the sense that of touch. The element symbolic of anahata is air.

5. *Vishuddhi*. This chakra is the centre of communication, as well as that of purification, as we move into a higher state of consciousness and awareness. This purification of mind enables us to discriminate between that which is of a more realized and awakened nature and that which is of a more gross and selfish nature. It is the purification of opposites and dualities into the awareness of oneness, for here the perception of both pleasure and pain are seen as a part of the whole and are consumed within the one. From vishuddhi is spoken and communicated this level of perception and understanding; there is a sweetness in our voice and words, and when we speak it is with truth. Through this centre thought vibrations from others are also received. Sound is a means to spiritual awakening through Kirtan and Bhajan (Indian chanting). When we chant this centre is activated.

Vishuddhi is located directly behind the throat pit. It is represented by a sixteen-petalled lotus that is purple in colour. The sound associated with vishuddhi is 'HAM', and the sense that of hearing. The element symbol of vishuddhi is ether.

6. *Ajna*. This sixth chakra is that of intuitive understanding and insight, often referred to as the Third Eye. Here we are reaching far greater realization that is not dependent on mundane knowledge. It is an intoxicated expansiveness, a joyfulness and a knowing of deep peace. There is light and great bliss. This is the opening of the third eye, the one that looks within to the inherent wisdom and to the inner guru, rather than looking outward for answers. Attachment to matter and form dissolve; there is complete transcendence of duality, of separate self. We awake from the dream.

Many spiritual seekers have had glimpses of truth, if only for a split second. One taste of this bliss is enough to reinforce our purpose to continue on the path towards realization. As enlightenment is our true nature we are unconsciously guided through this chakra in our impetus to see clearly. It is through our meditation, sincerity and genuine effort that we awaken this level of perception; through surrender we enter into this superconscious realm.

Ajna is located in the centre of the eyebrows, corresponding to the very top of the spinal cord. It is represented by a two-petalled lotus that is a translucent grey/silver colour. The sound associated to ajna is 'OM'. The element symbolic of ajna is mind.

7. *Bindu.* Some schools of thought only mention seven major chakras (the above six and sahasrara, below). But in traditional texts there is also another chakra, the bindu. This is the seat of nectar at the back and uppermost part of the head, where the Hindu priests have a tuft of hair. When this nectar is flowing, sweet energy is felt, nourishing the whole human system. This is known to revitalize the cells of the body and to keep us youthful. It is the nectar of the awakened mind, the nectar of truth; the source from which all creation comes, and into which all creation finally goes back. It is connected to vishuddhi chakra, and when vishuddhi is awakened so is bindu.

The bindu is located at the top of the head at the back. It is represented by the symbol of a crescent moon on a moonlit night. There are many sounds, but no particular one sound or element associated with bindu.

8. *Sahasrara.* This highest level of the chakras is where we awaken to full consciousness. It is the emancipation from the illusive nature of the lower realms, the merging into full realization. Here there is pure ecstasy and all desires are consumed. We are free of the cycle of birth and rebirth and our purpose for being alive is for the sake of all sentient beings. Our consciousness has expanded to infinity. This is true enlightenment.

Sahasrara is located at the crown of the head. It is represented by a thousand-petalled lotus flower that is bright red in colour.

7

From Relaxation to Realization

Through the practice of ICR we not only learn how to relax but we also have the opportunity to transform our personality from within. Such transformation takes place as we release the inner stresses and tensions and discover our inherent peace of mind. When we are severely stressed we are being influenced by emotional and mental conflicts that have accumulated in our minds; when we are relaxed we are in a naturally self-possessed state. Relaxation is therefore necessary as a prelude to going deeper in meditation. In this way knowledge of truth can arise as we are fully present and spontaneous, neither focusing on the past nor being concerned about the future. Truth can be revealed as we reside in a space of simply being.

Relaxing in this way takes courage as it involves a letting go of repetitive and compulsive behaviour. It is a path of maturity and awareness. As mature people we can begin to take greater responsibility for ourselves and our actions, for our influence and effect in the world. We can have more positive attitudes and make clearer choices. Events in themselves are neither good nor bad, they just are; it is our response to them that will make them either positive or negative experiences. By going deeper we see what is happening more objectively and can thus be free of the stress and distress caused by subjective involvement.

When life is going along smoothly it is easy to smile, but when events erupt our attitude is different. If someone hurts us, or causes abuse, can we still feel OK? We are constantly confronted with situations that bring up anger, frustration or rage. So on the one hand we want to be genuine, we practise and work with our limitations – and suddenly we are confronted with wanting to shout or hit someone! If we respond creatively and positively then the incident can often end there and the cause of that suffering is finished; by understanding the consequences of negativity, we begin to grow in awareness. It is important to see the humour in this whole process, for without a sense of humour we are truly doomed! It takes enormous self-control and skill to work with our emotions, so let us be humorous, as well as patient and gentle with ourselves. Seeing the wisdom in not reacting but in creatively responding to situations can only bring greater freedom.

Pain and suffering

Pain is inevitable, as we are fragile and vulnerable beings, but suffering is not. The way we relate to pain and our attitude towards it is essential to our development. The Master Sivananda of Rishikesh used to say, 'Pain and suffering, I welcome you!' I am not saying we should look for pain, but if it enters our lives then we can face it, bear it, and try to accept it as a teaching. We can see what it is we need to learn, rather than becoming a helpless victim of it. Swami Sivananda welcomed pain as a means of removing the causes of suffering, and as a way to teach us how to deal with our clinging and attachment to form. In the Buddhist teachings there is a practice called Tong Lin. Tong means giving and Lin means taking; so here the practitioner takes in the suffering of others so that they may be free of it, and gives out his own happiness so that others may benefit. In this way true selflessness can develop.

How we live each moment is an example of how aware we are of the truth. If we understand the law of karma, of cause and effect, it will help us to appreciate that when we become ill or are in a difficult situation, some past action is now ripening; even if we do not know what that action was, we can know that we are working through our own past deeds and releasing them. What is important is that we need not cause ourselves further suffering. By having the right understanding we can relate to our lives and our awakening with clearer intentions and live more harmoniously. For instance, when positive things happen to us – perhaps a financial success – we can see this success as a result of past positive activity and we can do more good with it, benefiting others in whatever way is appropriate. The old way would have been to think how special I am, or how superior I must be because I am so lucky, or how successful I am because I know more than others do, but this attitude only perpetuates ego-centred energy and will eventually bring pain. Opening our understanding to the laws that govern man, such as that of karma, brings a greater level of freedom in our daily activities.

Transformation

All the different techniques we may practise become integrated into our moment-to-moment understanding. We prepare our bed by cleaning and straightening the sheets, tidying it up and making it ready to get into at night. We get into it, but then sleep comes of its own. In the same way, our practice is a way of training the mind, a way of preparation, but without expectations. A breakthrough may come of its own, when everything drops away and we are naked with our truth. It is a knowing more beautiful than any other knowing and we are serene, peaceful and content; our lives can then become a service, a sharing and a blessing. This breakthrough may come in a flash or it may be a gentle waking up, as if our eyes now see more brightly and the clouds disperse so that the sun is shining. When this happens it feels as if it was never any different. It is a familiarity like coming home from a long journey and feeling immediately comfortable. It is an experience we can all have.

To transform means to be open to change, to have a creative attitude, and then to let that change permeate our every cell. To see that what may have been good for us today can be different tomorrow; not to have a fixed view of people or things, but to be compassionate and generous, with an open heart. Let us not become narrow-minded or think that what we have learnt is superior to another's understanding. We are not given the teachings so that we may become superior; the teachings are there to encourage our humility and simplicity. Our awakening is for the benefit of all beings, not just ourselves. True growth and transformation is a movement away from egotistical behaviour towards the altruistic.

Are we growing, are we learning? Are we deluding ourselves thinking we have done a certain amount of austere and advanced practice? Are we still causing pain? Do we feel superior? What I often see is puffed up spiritual egos, proud of all their hard work! Are we suffering from thinking that we know it all? If we have gained some insight then let us live it, be it. Do we have a sense of humour? Can we laugh at ourselves? Are we humble, simple, forgiving? We are here to enjoy life and laugh at its paradoxes, to accept what happens as lessons to be learnt and not to get too caught up in results. The greatest joy comes from knowing our own true Self and serving others. Peace of mind can never be bought. So as our attitudes change and we feel an inner happiness, we will know the direction we are going in is the right one. Our lives beome much sweeter, for simplicity is elegance.

Life is a game

As Plato said, 'Life must be lived as play.' Life is a game, to be enjoyed, and we are all players. With this in mind the way we live can be seen with a softness and ease, which is quite refreshing. We are only on this planet for such a short time and no doubt many things are going to happen, but if we can see it as an adventure then we can surely make this journey a truly masterful one. When we discover the wisdom that is beyond the analytical, rational mind we find it is not an intellectual knowing that will solve life's mysteries, but a deeper knowing, one that arises from a union of the heart and the mind. In this case the heart is our essential nature, unfiltered by thoughts and opinions. It is contacting that truth that is the inner guru, or guide. As Lao Tzu so eloquently put it in the *Tao te Ching*:

> There is no need to run outside
> For better seeing,
> Nor to peer from a window. Rather abide
> At the centre of your being;
> For the more you leave it, the less you
> learn.
> Search your heart and see
> If he is wise who takes each turn;
> The way to do is to be.

The realization of the truth, our highest intelligence, our essence, passes all understanding. This means that our ordinary faculties, the way we normally perceive things to be, merge into a greater knowing. By letting go, by surrendering our smallness, we realize that we are going through a transformation; as a butterfly emerges from its cocoon, we emerge out of the belief that we are an identity separate from the universal intelligence, into the awareness of unity. When all the information and programming of this computer-like mind, and all our concepts of self and other than self, drop away and we are in the moment, then we may see ourselves in all our glory as infinite love, infinite beauty and fully awake. As the *Bhagavad Gita* says, 'In the complete cessation of thought comes the precious gift of spiritual illumination.'

All of the world's religions are, in essence, expressions of this truth. The wise ones have come to remind us that we can discover for ourselves this universal message. No one can do it for us. Even mothers and fathers have to work hard to prepare their child to go out on his or her own and face the world with the strength and understanding to survive. They cannot do it *for* the child – they are there simply to support and encourage. The teachers, like our parents, are the ones who inspire. We won't find the truth in the various religions, for the truth is within, but the teachings are there to support our journey. Even books and scriptures are only signposts. It is through our own experience and innermost feelings that we can know, and that knowing is when we are alone with ourselves. Then we can awaken. The teachings of the wise ones are their gift to humanity: to thine own self be true. This was not said so that we would mistrust each other, but so that we would have faith in ourselves. Salvation comes from letting go of the ignorance that binds us and realizing this simple truth.

Lao Tzu said in the *Tao te Ching*, 'Those who were good practisers of Tao did not use it to make people bright, but rather used it to make them simple.' Our understanding is expressed in everything we do, say and are, and is a reflection of that which is deep within us, free from labels. The truth is without name and form – it is being without being anything. We have been taught since childhood to believe that God is invisible, but if we look carefully at what we are saying then we may see that God is in-visible – that by looking within ourselves we find that God is visible within.

Opening the heart

We can live in this world as the lotus flower that rises up from the mud. Although it comes from the mud its flower is clean and untainted by that mud. Our mud is made up of the limitations we need to transform in order to see the light of day. The practices we work with, such as ICR, are the tools, the means, we use to clear a way through the mud, to enable such change to occur. And we can emerge free of our conditioned mind, untainted by it. All the effort we have made is important, is meaningful, is not in vain. For all that we have done has led us to this point, has brought us to this understanding. The truth is always shining, and it may not be through any one effort but through all efforts that we see this. Each and every moment contributes to a new way of thinking, saying and being, and as we emerge from the mud our vision is clear and bright.

With our effort comes an opening of our hearts. The heart can be likened to a king, and the mind is like the king's adviser. The mind, the adviser, is the one who goes out and explores the world, searching and finding out what is happening. It then comes back to the king and reports on its findings. The king makes his decision, but he may choose a completely different path or activity from the one advised, and his decision may even seem irrational in light of the situation at hand. But the king has a greater view. He sees from all sides and knows what is the overall good. In the same way we can turn to and trust our inner king. We can allow our hearts to speak to us and guide us.

Our purpose is to expand our minds and, to open our hearts so that we may fully enter into life. No particular technique will necessarily give this to us, but the attitude we have is what is important. Are we being kind? Are we truly loving ourselves? Are we being judgemental? Are we being compassionate? Our awakening can be measured by our fearlessness in being naked to the truth, exposed, non-clinging, and free of the superficial; by being humble and knowing we are blessed. We are always in grace. We are beautiful reflections of a living presence that is guiding us from within. The transformation that we experience is a process of identifying with unity, not with the limited understanding of separate self. We are all on our own journey, the ultimate purpose of which is to awaken by realizing the truth of our existence, for only then can we be of real use to ourselves and to others.

Awakening from the drama of life

> Our birth is but a sleep and a forgetting;
> The Soul that rises with us, our life's Star,
> Hath had elsewhere its setting,
> And cometh from afar.
>
> Not in entire forgetfulness
> And not in utter nakedness
> But trailing clouds of glory do we come
> From God, who is our home.
>
> WORDSWORTH

All the great teachers in the different ages have spoken of this state of being that is beyond duality. In this state we are not affected by the limitations we find each day in our pursuit for happiness. Ramana Maharashi, one of India's greatest masters, constantly told the thousands who came to him for his teachings, 'Enquire "Who am I?" and keep pursuing this until you realize.' Discovering this simple truth for ourselves creates the underlying joy of our entire existence. Nothing can make us happier than this knowledge, as it is the very foundation of our inner Self. All other knowledge comes from this.

Ramana Maharashi compared this world to the drama that takes place in a cinema. Before the movie plays the screen is blank – it is clear and white. Then the lights go out, the projector is turned on and the drama begins. We laugh and cry and feel all sorts of emotions, and then when the film is over we see the blank white screen again. In life we live the drama and get caught up in the story. We forget that it is simply a drama, that our true Self is the screen that the drama of life is being played on. It is up to us to awake from this drama and realize our joyful, radiant Self, free from pain and sorrow, profit and loss.

The Master Swami Vivekananda said, 'Learn to live in this world but be not of it.' By being peaceful and untainted by the dualities in life we can relate fully to our everyday existence, yet also be free. It's not as if we are not challenged or do not face difficulties. Of course we do – but we do not have to identify with the difficulties. If we trust our inner wisdom, then we can learn to deal calmly with whatever happens. Instead of getting panicked and fearful, we can act from a place of truth. The difference between knowing and not knowing depends upon our perception. When we perceive clearly, then we develop a loving and compassionate understanding. This is a knowing that is experienced when the mind is still. Through such knowing our lives become an expression of compassion and love and a reflection of the truth.

Attitude and motivation

As we move from a state of unknowing to one of knowing it is helpful to understand the qualities of those who have gone beyond limited self-serving attitudes to a greater vision. The nature of those who have realized this vision is hard to describe in words, for they have infinite understanding, light and wisdom. They appear confident and are skilful without bringing pain. But they are also elusive! The Buddha said that such beings may appear as wise men, ghosts, children or even madmen!

Getting close to such beings can be difficult, because they are not with us to pamper our egos but act as a reflection to show us what we need to see in ourselves. So sometimes it may be painful to be with them, but this pain is also exquisite as it is an intimate form of growing pains. As the teachers are coming from a place of oneness they have no selfish motives; their only concern is to help us to awaken a state of clarity. A good teacher is a true friend. When we are with such beings we feel we never want to leave. It is like coming home after a long time away, to our long-lost nearest and dearest. The enlightened mind is not limited to any particular way of thinking because this state is beyond thought; the wisdom that comes from such awareness is beneficial towards the transformation of all. In witnessing their impartial understanding we may feel safe to surrender our ego-centred attitudes. To be thus inspired gives our lives meaning and helps remove the doubts that so often creep into our roaming minds.

Those who embody loving kindness want all beings to have happiness and those things that cause them happiness. Through loving kindness we can transform our ignorance and we find we are wishing good fortune even for our enemies! As Master Sivananda said, 'Our enemies are our friends and our friends are our enemies.' For our friends support us in our neurosis, while our enemies show us our limitations. We can then see that the bringing of pain to another is an act born out of ignorance, that it is due to believing there is a difference between us, instead of seeing that we are one. Our enemies are not our enemies, for they are simply acting out of a limited understanding and know no better. We can develop an attitude of forgiveness and loving kindness, and thereby rid ourselves of unnecessary misery, for in forgiveness there is

freedom. Compassion is the wish that all beings might be free
from suffering and those things that cause suffering. This
quality helps to purify our minds and clears away the
negativity. If we put ourselves in the place of others and
others in our place, then we can be sensitive and helpful to
what is truly needed.

Our motivation is important, because this allows for
wisdom and compassion to emerge. To have an impartial
view of life is a great virtue, for this approach implies the
ability to go through the obstacles to see the truth beyond
them. Peace is the state of being that is our true nature. It is
not something new or outside, it is always with us. But just as
we cannot see our face unless we look in a mirror, so we do
not see our peace. Only when we no longer identify with the 'I
consciousness', with 'I, me, mine and other', can we realize
our peace.

Associating with and meeting people who are consciously
making an effort to change is an important way to encourage
growth and realization. People who support each other in
skilful acts inspire further effort. It is especially helpful if we
are working through difficult times. If one of us is strong and
another is in a vulnerable state, then our positive influence
may be all that is needed to reinforce the other's convictions
and to enable movement to occur through the difficulty. We
are not alone in our quest for truth, and the sharing that
comes from group effort is very powerful. The Buddha talked
about the spiritual community as being a great 'jewel', to be
treasured and honoured as precious to our growth. Coming
together to meditate, to have discussions and to share in each
other's joy helps us see more clearly. How we view ourselves
is not always the way that others see us, and issues that arise
in such relationships can help us become more aware of our
limitations.

As we aspire towards realization we make a deeper
commitment to our awakening. By doing this we attract those
situations that will further our development. The practices
that we do, such as Inner Conscious Relaxation, should be
done with one-pointedness and the belief that we will succeed.
With a willingness to move beyond our limitations and by
clearly discriminating between that which is skilful and that

which is unskilful, we further our motivation. All our effort helps remove the hindrances that hold us back. Remembering our true purpose for taking birth, and the blessings we have received in being shown the way to go, gives us strength to draw on at all times.

Being at peace

The practice of relaxation and meditation can take us beneath the superficial layers that obscure the mind, to a place of serenity, clarity and peace. It is an opportunity to be in the present moment with no clinging or attachment to our thinking. When the mind is thus calm and peaceful we are able to be content within the moment. Nothing else exists. It is a natural state that radiates joy. Many great Indian teachers were illiterate, but their devotion and sincere motivation to awaken were genuine. Their unswerving faith and surrender cut through the veils of ignorance to the knowledge that is not based on anything, is free and arises spontaneously. This is known as non-abidance, to reside in no one place and is impermanent, without reference points. To be free, enlightened, is to realize that there is actually no mind. Rather we are pure Self that is ever-blissful.

When we practise meditation with the proper motivation then our concern is not just for personal peace, but for all beings to have peace. As we see truth within ourselves, we see it in others and wish for their awakening. This is the realization that within all beings lies the potential to awaken to their true nature. As we deepen our understanding it becomes natural to dedicate our practice and our understanding for the benefit of all beings.

The underlying purpose of ICR is not only relaxation but to also awaken to the many dimensions of consciousness; to release our attachments to the world and enter into the realm of meditation. A natural healing occurs as energy is released from its fixed patterns, and this enables us to experience the awakened state more fully. Then there is no difference between one level and another, and the universe is not only seen as a living whole but is deeply and personally realized within. This state is the integration of the universal mind, where everything drops away and we experience our true nature. Then there is no difference between within and without. The fullest expression of ICR is therefore the illumination of the unconscious to reveal the superconscious state. This is where inner conscious relaxation becomes inner conscious realization.

> We shall not cease from exploration
> And the end of our exploring
> Will be to arrive where we started
> And know the place for the first
> time.
>
> T. S. ELIOT

8

The Practice

The purpose of practice is to bring about a state of ease and deep relaxation, as well as that of insight and realization. It is a process of taming the mind and of making friends with ourselves. Inner Conscious Relaxation is a means to relax with full conscious awareness. It is a means to realizing our greater aspirations by cutting through the layers of delusion; thus eliminating the deep mental impressions, samskaras, that are the root of our doubts and confusion. In the relative sense we therefore work with purifying the obscurities of the mind, in order to reach the ultimate level.

We do not always have time to learn and practise the rigours of yogic philosophy or other disciplines, yet we suffer from mental tension and the inability to relax. It is important to relax deeply. As we learn to let go in this way, we can empower our lives to go in the direction which will be most fulfilling. The practices in this chapter are designed to enable us to open ourselves to the natural state of realization already within us. The music is there; we just have to learn how to listen.

In this age of awakening it is natural to feel the true joy of our own nature. It is not mysterious or even difficult to understand. It doesn't take intelligence, just a willingness to be happy and give up the struggle of trying to get something.

We have it! We are it! But we get stuck, our minds and bodies get tense. So let us practise away the pressures that build up each day and be cheerful. What seemed impossible yesterday can be realized today!

General instructions

We can practise ICR in a number of ways, alone or in a group. We can either record the following instructions on to a cassette recorder to play back to ourselves; or we can have a friend read them while we listen. The ICR practice is also available on cassette tape from Element Books. In either case the instructions should be read slowly, or more quickly when it is indicated. There are also times when we pause between each direction. This is important. When we feel we know the practice well enough it can be done without any outside help. The instructions are simple; just follow them carefully and enjoy the process. At the beginning and end of the practice we will be repeating the resolve, so it is helpful to have already formulated our own resolve.

When practising ICR we wear loose, comfortable clothing and do it in a space where we will not be interrupted. The practice lasts approximately half an hour and can be adjusted to suit the amount of time available. In these practices we want to listen to the instruction without interruption and without going to sleep. If we have insomnia and our minds are chattering away, or we are preoccupied with the problems of the day and need to sleep, at those times we can practise just for that reason.

The first part of the practice can also be used at any time of the day to bring about relaxation as it is needed. It can be done by sitting in a chair for a few minutes so that physical and mental tensions are released and we are refreshed. To do this, relax the body mentally as in the first practice, followed by the breathing instructions.

ICR practices are normally done lying down; in this position it is easier to relax. It is especially beneficial if we find it difficult to sit still in an upright position. But the way we want to practise is up to each of us to decide. Sometimes we may want to lie down but seem to fall asleep and can't finish the practice. If that is the case, then we should sit upright and see how it feels. At other times sitting can be distracting as our bodies ache and we want to lie down. What is needed is the right attitude and the interest to practise.

When we practise ICR lying on the floor we put a blanket or a mat beneath us. We can have a thin pillow under our heads and a light blanket covering us. We lie down on our backs; our arms are parallel at our sides, a few inches from the body, with the palms facing upwards. The legs are comfortably apart. If we need to we can sit with our spine upright, either cross-legged on the floor or in a straight-backed chair. Our hands should be palms upright in our laps. In a chair the feet should both be flat on the floor. We should be as comfortable as possible, wearing no jewellery or other distracting accessories (no watches or glasses). The eyes are closed. The room should be semi-dark and quiet, preferably with the windows and doors closed unless there is a need for air. The room should be neither too hot nor too cold, nor open to draughts or breezes. We may want to read through the practice first. Now we either switch on the tape we have of this practise, or we listen to the spoken instructions from a friend. We follow the instructions mentally. There is no need to concentrate or do anything other than listen and remember not to sleep. It is best to practise when we are alert and fully awake.

INNER CONSCIOUS RELAXATION

This is the most basic and comprehensive form of ICR. Before starting refer to General Instructions, above. Relax your body physically by making final adjustments to your posture. You must be absolutely still for the whole practice of Inner Conscious Relaxation.

The first phase

Now let us relax the body mentally. As you refer to the part of the body take your time, do not move quickly. Bring your mind to the tips of the feet and mentally move up the body from the feet...ankles...calves...knees...thighs.

Wherever there is tension release it. Move with the mind to the hips...waist...stomach...chest...shoulders...fingers...hands ...wrists...elbows...up to the shoulders.

Now to the back of the body...the buttocks...the back...then the neck...face and head. Now the whole body is relaxed mentally. Wherever there is tension let it go. Release and relax.

Do not sleep; just be aware of the voice instructing you and stay with the practice as best possible. Say to yourself mentally, 'I will not sleep'. There is no need for mental activity other than being aware and following the instruction. Whatever arises in the mind let it go. Just follow the practice. Whether thoughts, visions or any impressions arise in the mind, just let them go, just be with the practice. Mentally say to yourself, 'I am aware I am going to practice Inner Conscious Relaxation'. In the next few moments repeat this three times. During Inner Conscious Relaxation we are not aware of what is happening outside of us, nor are we asleep. It is in that space in-between that the practice takes place.

Become aware of the breathing process. Just let the breath enter and leave the nostril area, like a triangle with no base. The breath enters both nostrils and meets at the eyebrow centre, and then you exhale. Feel you are in the nostrils, take your awareness there and be aware of the breathing in and out. Do this for a few minutes.

Now let us become aware of the resolve. The resolve is a statement concerning your life. Something you want to come true. Something purposeful and meaningful that represents your life's aspirations. Resolves made in life may or may not come true, but the resolve made at the beginning of Inner Conscious Relaxation and repeated again at the end will come true. It should be a simple sentence with few punctuations. Repeat it three times to yourself over the next few moments.

The second phase

The next phase of Inner Conscious Relaxation is the rotation of consciousness. I will mention a part of the physical body, and you repeat and visualize that part in your mind, simultaneously becoming aware of that part. We move as quickly as possible. If it is easy to do, fine, and if not it is also OK. This is not concentration; just stay with the practice and do not sleep.

Become aware of the right thumb, second finger, third finger, fourth finger, fifth finger, palm of the right hand, back of the hand, right wrist, lower arm, elbow, upper arm, right shoulder, armpit, right side of the waist, hip, thigh, knee, calf, ankle, heel, sole of the right foot, ball of the right foot, big toe, second toe, third toe, fourth toe, fifth toe.

Become aware of the left thumb, second finger, third finger, fourth finger, fifth finger, palm of the left hand, back of the hand, left wrist, lower arm, elbow, upper arm, left shoulder, armpit, left side of the waist, hip, thigh, knee, calf, ankle, heel, sole of the left foot, ball of the left foot, big toe, second toe, third toe, fourth toe, fifth toe.

Now become aware of the right shoulder blade, the left shoulder blade, the spinal cord, the right buttock, the left buttock, and the whole of the back together.

Become aware of the navel, the abdomen, the right side of the chest, the left side of the chest, the hollow of the chest, the well of the neck, the neck, chin, upper lip, lower lip, both lips together, right cheek, left cheek, nose, nose tip, right ear, left ear, right temple, left temple, right eye, left eye, right eyelid, left eyelid, right eyebrow, left eyebrow, centre of the eyebrows, forehead, top of the head, the whole body, the whole body, the whole body. Say to yourself mentally, 'I am aware of the whole of my physical body.' Please do not sleep, do not sleep! Remain aware of the practice and keep listening to the voice.

We now repeat this rotation of consciousness through the body again.

The third phase

The next phase of Inner Conscious Relaxation is being aware of the opposites, starting with the feeling of heaviness. Awaken the feeling of heaviness in the body, awaken the feeling of heaviness. Gather the particles of energy that create heaviness and feel heaviness in the whole of the physical body. What is heaviness? A lead weight that is hard to lift. Feel so heavy that you are sinking into the floor. Spend a few moments being heavy.

Now awaken the feeling of lightness. What is lightness? Awaken the feeling of lightness in your body as if you are resting on a cloud. Awaken lightness. Gather the particles of energy that create lightness and let the body experience lightness. Experience a few moments feeling lightness.

Now let us experience coldness in the whole body. What is coldness? It is a snowy, winter's day and you are walking barefoot in the snow. The whole body is cold, very cold. There is a chill going up the spine. The feet are cold, the legs, arms, body and head are cold. Gather the particles of energy that produce coldness and experience coldness in the whole body. Your whole body feels cold. Spend a few moments feeling coldness.

Now we experience heat. What is heat? It is a hot summer's day, you are on the beach and want to go into the water. The sand is too hot, you are sweating. Feel heat in the whole of the physical body. Gather the particles of energy that produce heat and feel heat in the whole body. Your whole body is hot. Experience heat for a few moments.

Now pain. What is pain? An experience from the past? Gather the energy particles of pain and feel pain in one part of the physical body or the whole of the physical body. Intensify the feeling of pain, either in one part or the whole of the physical body. Get into the feeling of pain. Spend a few moments feeling pain.

Now what is pleasure? Something you feel right now? Maybe something from the past, an experience of great pleasure. Gather the particles of energy and bring the feeling of pleasure into the moment and feel pleasure. Spend a few moments feeling pleasure.

Stay with the practice! If the mind drifts, bring it back to the practice and do the best you can. No sleeping! Be aware that you are practising.

The fourth phase

The next phase of Inner Conscious Relaxation is the awareness of the energy centres, the chakras. In our being there are energy centres. They are not physical but psychic, and therefore on a higher plane. They have a name and a symbol and can be located at certain points along the spinal region. Let us take our minds to where they are located and repeat the name of the centre and then try to visualize the symbol. Let us try to awaken these centres. We start at the base and move upwards, pausing between each one.

Mooladhara is the first chakra and is located in men at the perineum, between the anus and the scrotum and half an inch inside. In women it is at the cervix, half an inch inside. The symbol is a red inverted triangle with a pink serpent in it, with three and a half coils, its head looking downwards and with the fangs coming from its mouth. Take your mind to that point, at the perineum in men and the cervix in women. Repeat mentally three times, 'Mooladhara, mooladhara, mooladhara', and visualize this symbol.

Swadhisthana is the second chakra and is located at the base of the spine in the coccyx. The symbol is unconsciousness. Visualize the endless sea in the dark night. Take your mind to that point, at the base of the spine. Repeat mentally three times, 'Swadhisthana, swadhisthana, swadhisthana', and visualize the symbol.

Manipura is the third chakra and is located in the spinal cord at the level of the navel. The symbol is a yellow sunflower. Take your mind to that point, at the level of the navel in the spinal cord. Repeat mentally three times, 'Manipura, manipura, manipura', and visualize the yellow sunflower.

Anahata is the fourth chakra and is located at the hollow of the chest in the spinal cord. The symbol is a small candle flame. Take your mind to that point, at the impression of the chest in the spinal cord. Repeat mentally three times, 'Anahata, anahata, anahata', and visualize the small flame of a candle.

Vishuddhi is the fifth chakra and is located at the well of the neck in the spinal cord. The symbol is cold drops of nectar. Take your mind to that point, at the well of the neck in the spinal cord, Repeat mentally three times, 'Vishuddhi, vishuddhi, vishuddhi', and visualize cold drops of nectar.

Ajna is the sixth chakra and is located at the level of the centre of the eyebrows, looking from within. The symbol is the feeling of intoxication, as if drunk with bliss, and this is where the intuition is awakened. Take your mind to the point between the eyebrows from the inside and focus. Repeat mentally three times, 'Ajna, ajna, ajna', and feel the bliss of intoxication.

Bindu is the seventh chakra and is located at the back and top of the head, diagonally opposite the chin, where the Hindus and Krishna devotees wear a small tuft of hair. The symbol is a crescent moon in a moonlit night. Take your mind to the back and top of the head. Repeat mentally three times, 'Bindu, bindu, bindu', and visualize a crescent moon in a moonlit night.

Sahasrara is the eighth chakra and is situated at the crown of the head, about an inch inside. The symbol is one petal of a thousand-petalled red lotus flower. One petal is much bigger than your head. Take your mind to the crown of the head one inch inside. Repeat mentally three times, 'Sahasrara, sahasrara, sahasrara', and visualize one petal of the thousand-petalled lotus much bigger than your head.

Stay with the practice, be aware of it and do not sleep.

We will now rotate our awareness through the chakras or psychic centres, touching each centre with our minds trying to visualize the symbol and going up and down the spine. We go to the point, repeat the name, try to visualize the symbol and then move on. If it is difficult to visualize the symbol, just bring your mind to the chakra centre mentally, repeat the name and move on to the next, going up and down touching each centre with the mind. Mooladhara at perineum in men, cervix in women, swadhisthana at the base of the spine, manipura navel centre in spine, anahata hollow of the chest in the spine, vishuddhi well of the neck in the spine, ajna at the level of the centre of the eyebrows from the inside, bindu diagonally opposite the chin, sahasrara at the crown of the head from the inside. Now downward: sahasrara, bindu, ajna, vishuddhi, anahata, manipura, swadhisthana, mooladhara.

Repeat once again, going up and down the energy centres a little faster: mooladhara, swadhisthana, manipura, anahata, vishuddhi, ajna, bindu, sahasrara; sahasrara, bindu, ajna, vishuddhi, anahata, manipura, swadhisthana, mooladhara.

Now go to the head area in the centre of the brain. Focus your awareness there. Visualize a tiny golden egg. There is a golden egg, a tiny golden egg. Understand your higher Self as that tiny golden egg. Spend a few minutes with this.

Then repeat the resolve that you made at the beginning of the practice. Repeat the resolve three times. Become aware of the breath without effort, as it enters and leaves your body. Stay with this for a few moments. Now become aware of your physical body, your feet, legs, arms, trunk, shoulders and head. Move the body gently and become aware of the room you are in. Take your time, and make sure your consciousness is externalized. Roll on your side, take a few breaths, then sit up, open your eyes and have a smile on your face.

GUIDED VISUALIZATION

This Inner Conscious Relaxation practice is based on specific visualization. Before starting see the general instructions, on page 88. Relax your body physically by making final adjustments. Now be absolutely still for the whole practice.

Let us first relax the body mentally. As you mention the part of the body take your time and do not move quickly. Bring your mind to the tips of the feet and mentally move up the body from the feet...ankles...calves...knees...thighs. Wherever there is tension, release it. Move with the mind to the hips...waist...stomach...chest...fingers...hands...wrists... elbows...up to the shoulders...the back of the body... buttocks...back...then the neck...face...and the head. Now the whole body is relaxed mentally. Wherever there is tension, let it go.

Do not sleep, just be aware of the voice instructing you and stay with the practice. Say to yourself mentally, 'I will not sleep.' There is no need for mental activity other than being aware and following the instruction. Whatever arises in the mind, let it go; just follow the practice. If thoughts, visions or impressions arise in the mind, let them go; just be with the practice. Mentally say to yourself, 'I am aware I am going to practise Inner Conscious Relaxation', and repeat this mentally three times for the next few moments. In Inner Conscious Relaxation we are not aware of what is happening outside of us, nor are we asleep. It is in that space between that the practice takes place.

Now become aware of the breathing process. Just let the breath enter and leave the nostril area, like a triangle with no base. The breath enters both nostrils, meets at the eyebrow centre, so take your awareness there and be aware of the breathing in and out. Do this for a few minutes.

Now let us become aware of the resolve. The resolve is a statement concerning your life. Something you want to come true. Something that is purposeful and meaningful, that is your life's aspiration. Resolves made in life may or may not come true but the resolve made at the beginning and repeated again at the end of Inner Conscious Relaxation will come true. It is a simple sentence with few punctuations. Kindly repeat it three times to yourself for the next few moments.

Become aware of the meeting point of the left leg and the ground. Bring your mind to that point and concentrate. Take a few moments to do this.

Now bring your awareness to the meeting point of the right leg and the ground and concentrate there for a few moments.

Bring your awareness to the meeting point between the left arm and the ground and concentrate in that area for a few moments.

Bring your awareness to the meeting point between your right arm and the ground and concentrate there for a few moments.

Now bring your awareness to the meeting point between your whole back and the ground and concentrate in that area for a few moments. Then bring your awareness to the meeting point between the back of the head and the ground and concentrate there for a few moments.

Finally become aware of the meeting point of the whole body and the ground and concentrate in that area for a few moments.

Do not sleep! Be aware that you are practising Inner

Conscious Relaxation!

Now I will create a visualization and you should try to bring it into the mind as best as you can. Do not try to concentrate; just see what comes to you and move without trying too hard. You can visualize it any way you can, going from one image to the next. Move with awareness.

Red rose * a child riding a bicycle on the road * a plane flying over head * clouds in the sky * grey clouds * blue clouds * your physical body * you outside your physical body looking down at your body * a camel with two humps * a newborn baby * the Virgin Mary * a yogi sitting in meditation * a candle burning * the ocean * waves breaking on the shore * a person rowing on a lake * the ripples from the oars * a church * inside the church a preacher is giving a sermon * a golden cross * a dog barking * your physical body lying on the ground naked and a golden thread going upward from your navel * the Buddha * a palm tree * an oak tree * a large balloon high up in the sky * a mouse * a nun * a Christmas tree * a dead body * a policeman * the waves of the ocean * people sunbathing on the beach * a church choir * snow-capped mountains * a river rushing after a rainstorm.

Now let us travel to a faraway island. It is a tropical island with lush trees and vegetation. On the island live many animals: lions, tigers, snakes, elephants, zebra and deer. They all live in peace. In the centre of the island is a grass hut. A yogi sits outside the hut in a cross-legged meditation pose. A fire is burning next to him. Smoke is emanating from it and the smell of incense is everywhere. The sound of 'om' can be heard. There is a quiet peace.

Now become aware of the resolve. Mentally repeat three times the resolve that you made at the beginning of the practice. Repeat it, knowing it will come true.

Become aware of the breath. Watch the breath enter and leave the physical body with no effort. Now become aware of the physical body: the legs, trunk, arms and head. See yourself lying on the floor with your eyes closed. When you are ready, roll to the side, sit up and open your eyes.

CHAKRA VISUALIZATION

The following meditation involves the use of visualization and awareness of the chakras to help us expand our awareness and heighten our understanding of these levels of perception. Each of the chakras has a specific sound vibration that is repeated mentally and a particular lotus flower that we visualize. By repeating the sound we can become more in tune with these levels of perception. This particular practice may be done while sitting up rather than lying on the floor. Before starting refer to the General Instructions, page 88.

Now become aware of the physical body being still, with no movement. Take a few minutes to relax completely.

Experience the physical body sitting in the centre of a white lotus flower, a beautiful white lotus flower. It is very large and your physical form is in the centre. Visualize a white lotus flower and your form is in the centre. Thoughts may enter the mind but let them go. Gently, give no power to the thoughts but just keep visualizing the form and being in the centre of the lotus flower. Stay with this for a few minutes.

Now bring your awareness to the breath. Watch it enter and leave the body. As each breath enters it is nourishing the whole body and opening your being. Feel you are opening. Mentally say, 'I am opening.' As you exhale it is helping to let go. Feel you are letting go. Mentally say, 'I am letting go.' Stay with the breath, being aware of the breath and getting closer until the mind and the breath unite. Feel you are one with the breath, opening up and letting go.

When you feel you are united with the breath for some time bring your awareness to the chakras, the consciousness centres in the body.

Mooladhara is located in men at the perineum between the anus and the scrotum, and in women in the cervix, both half an inch inward. Concentrate the mind at this point and mentally repeat the sound 'LAM' while visualizing a red lotus with four petals. Take a few moments to do this.

Swadhisthana is located at the base of the spine. Concentrate the mind at this point and mentally repeat the sound 'VAM' while visualizing an orange-red lotus with six petals for the next few moments.

Manipura is located in the spine at the level of the navel. Concentrate the mind at this point and mentally repeat the sound 'RAM' while you visualize a yellow lotus with ten petals for the next few moments.

Anahata is located at the hollow of the chest in the spine. Concentrate the mind at this point and mentally repeat the sound 'YAM' while you visualize a blue lotus with twelve petals. As you focus there bring your breath to that region and feel the breath going in and out. Stay with the breath and visualization for a few minutes. This is the centre of love. Feel your love connecting with universal love. Feel that there is no difference between the love between you and all beings. Become aware as you concentrate at the heart centre that you are merging your love with cosmic love. Feel the expansiveness of your love merging into cosmic love. Stay with this for a few moments.

Vishuddhi is located at the well of the neck in the spine. Concentrate the mind at this point mentally and repeat the sound 'HAM' while you visualize a violet lotus with sixteen petals for the next few moments.

Ajna located at the centre of the eyebrows. Concentrate the mind at this point and mentally repeat the sound 'OM' while you visualize a smoky grey lotus with two petals. Bring the breath here and feel you are breathing in and out, awakening the feeling of bliss and intuition. Stay with this for a few moments.

As you experience this bliss, feel you are merging into cosmic consciousness that is infinitely blissful and full of light. Expand the light until it fills every cell of your body. See the light everywhere and visualize the whole planet in light. The whole planet is filled with cosmic light. Bathe in this light. Stay with this for the next few moments.

When you are ready, gently come out of the meditation.

THE WITNESS PRACTICE

In this practice, we develop our ability to witness our thoughts without getting subjectively involved. This Inner Conscious Relaxation technique is experiencing the body as the temple.

Before starting, see the general instructions on page 88.

We begin by relaxing the body physically, making all adjustments and then being still. We now relax the body mentally. Using the mind go to the feet and, moving upwards, remove tension wherever it lingers. The feet...calves...knees ...thighs...waist...hips...chest...shoulders...arms...neck... head.

Then become aware of the whole body. Experience the whole body as if it is your temple and stay focused on the form, the temple, for a few minutes.

Now become aware of the resolve. Make it a simple sentence and repeat it mentally three times. Let it express your true feelings concerning what you most want in life on a higher conscious level.

Again return to the body and experience it as if it is your temple, a place you can enter into to find peace and tranquillity. After a while begin to follow the breathing process. The breath enters both nostrils and then leaves, like a triangle without a base. Bring the mind and the breath together, getting closer and closer until they unite. Count the breaths at the end of each breath. Breathe in and breathe out and then count, starting with 27 and going backwards to 1. If you lose the count start again at 27. An inhalation and an exhalation is one count.

Stay with the practice and do not sleep.

Now become aware of the thoughts that enter and leave the mind. Whatever enters the mind it doesn't matter. If they are good or bad thoughts it doesn't matter. Just be the witness. Often what happens is that awful thoughts arise, and as we go deeper more pleasant thoughts come into the mind. Whatever happens, we do not get involved. Maintain the attitude of the witness. Under all circumstances you are the witness, simply watching what is taking place. So if you notice your mind drifting and you are getting involved with the thinking process, then mentally say 'Witness' to yourself and continue observing. We are not our thoughts, we are the witness. You may notice the mind becoming quieter. Observe the quiet mind for a few moments.

Again be aware and do not sleep. Stay with the practice for maximum success.

Bring your awareness to the centre of the eyebrows. Looking at the centre from the inside is darkness. In that darkness is a tiny light the size of a pin point. As you gaze at that point it will open. The feeling is blissful. Enjoy the bliss and stay with the light. If other images, colours or thoughts come forth, let them go. Just visualize the light for a few minutes.

Remember the resolve. Mentally repeat three times the resolve that you made at the beginning of the practice. Be aware and conscious, and feel it deeply!

Now become aware of the breathing process. Just let the breath enter and leave the physical body without doing anything. Feel relaxed and then become aware of your physical body. Your hands, arms, trunk of the body, legs and head. Gently move the parts as you become aware of the room. Externalize your awareness, and when you feel ready roll over on your side, then sit up and open your eyes.

SHORT PRACTICE FOR INSOMNIA

Usually Inner Conscious Relaxation is done for the purpose of relaxing or becoming aware of higher states of consciousness. The main instruction is not to sleep. But there are times when a person is so highly strung or the mind is so busy that sleep is difficult. In that case you can use the following practice, which is intended to help bring on sleep.

As you lie in bed face upwards, and have your arms next to your body, palms facing downwards, with your eyes closed. Rotate your consciousness through each part of the body, repeating the part to yourself and visualizing each part. This can be done a couple of times and relaxes the body and mind.

Next become aware of the breathing in the nostrils. Begin by counting down from 54 to 1, keeping the awareness from the tip of the nose to the eyebrow centre. An inhalation and an exhalation is one count. Breathe in, breathe out and count. If thoughts enter the mind, pay no attention to them; just keep following the breath. If you lose your way during the counting, then go back to 54. Sleep may come at any time during the practice. Good luck!

Eddie Shapiro's cassette tape, *Inner Conscious Relaxation*, is also available. Please contact your usual supplier or, in case of difficulty: Element Books Ltd, Longmead, Shaftesbury, Dorset, SP7 8PL, U.K.

Index